MY
OF MIND

A SCIENTIFIC ENQUIRY

SUNIL MISHRA

गरुड

Published by
Garuda Prakashan Private Limited
Gurugram, India

www.garudabooks.com

First published in India 2022

ISBN: 979-8-8857-5028-8

Cover Design: Pallavi Saxena

Printed in India

I dedicate this book to my father.

Contents

Foreword

We know that some topics are very mystical. On such topics, much has been discussed through ages, umpteen books have been written already, and even then, the discussion is not over. There is still an opportunity to present a refreshing point of view. Human mind is one among those topics that has intrigued us since beginning of mankind. The more we read or write about the same, the more we realize that we know so little about it. The scope is just too vast. There are useful wisdoms from the ancient texts of different civilizations that compete with modern scientific studies in the universities today. On the topic of human mind, I have found learnings from some of the ancient texts like Bhagvad Gita quite relevant even in the modern settings. I do quote them in the leadership sessions.

This complex topic has also been studied by different disciplines; be it theology, psychology, philosophy or brain science. Each discipline has its viii | Mysteries of Mind

own point of view with its own proponents and critiques. However, the debate is not settled yet and is unlikely to be settled anytime soon. Sunil's book *Mysteries of our Mind* is a unique attempt to blend different perspective from different disciplines. It presents the modern studies of neuroscience as well as Vedic perspectives on human mind. Definitely, there are some takeaways from each of these different perspectives.

The book covers topics like definition of self, search for happiness, memory, empathy, superstition, language, free will, mindfulness, procrastination, attention, emotions, illusion and future of mind in an era of artificial intelligence. The book also has some practical self-help tips on each of these topics. Sunil uses a logical and science-based approach to discuss these aspects. I am sure the readers will find this book interesting and useful.

—Professor Debashish Chatterjee

Director, IIM - Kozhikode

Preface

If our minds were easy to understand, we wouldn't have been so smart. Paradoxically, we try to use our intelligence to study what gives us intelligence, which is a daunting task. Human mind is such a complex topic that writing anything about it is more likely to be wrong than right. This inexact science is not even recognised as a formal discipline of study. It is said that in science, nothing can ever be proven to be absolute truth. It can only be proven 'not to be false' at a particular time. Hence, the fundamental principle of scientific theory is—'falsifiability', which means that any theory must run the risk of being proven wrong through counter experimentations. Newton's law is 'falsifiable' because tomorrow if someone comes with an observation that objects don't follow the law, we will have to junk those principles. For science, the thumb rule is very simple; if something can't be potentially wrong, it can never be right. Progressively, we pick the prevailing truths and falsify them to find out the new truths.

What can be said about the mind—is it falsifiable? We have never studied about the mind in our schools. Even for advanced medical science, the mind is a very nebulous topic; it is elusive. It is not governed by the natural laws of physics or biology. If you don't know the quantum theory, you will not be able to understand the sub-atomic world. Unfortunately, we don't yet have elementary tools to scientifically nail how the mind works. Since we don't know the alphabets, there is no way we can learn the language. With so many unknowns, the intellectual approach to address this topic has been to deny its existence, and that is why formal science almost never ventures into this territory. Scientists talk about the brain and stop at saying that the mind is a special construct of the brain, and it does not have its own existence.

Yet, we all know that the mind exists because we all experience it in our day-to-day life. The mind is like a torch with which we see the world around us; just that when we shine the spotlight back on this torch, we are blinded. Neuroscientists, philosophers, spiritual gurus, psychologists and commoners like us, all have tried to understand it from their own perspectives. Many have spent their lifetimes studying this topic, but we still don't have any definitive 'science of mind' yet. When it comes to the mind, experts are no different from the several blind people trying to describe an elephant by touching one part of its body at a time. We don't have anyone who has complete mastery on this subject, even though some may claim partial understanding.

It is important to bring out the finer differences of mind, brain and soul that are used interchangeably at times. There is no dispute about the brain—it has material existence. It can be touched, felt and studied. It is like computer hardware. The mind on the other hand is the software of the brain. We can't deny its existence, but at the same time we do not know enough to study it. The soul is the extreme end of the spectrum that only the religions acknowledge. Formal science has consistently refuted those claims of the soul.

Let me start with a disclaimer that I am not a neuroscientist, spiritual guru or any credited psychologist. At best, I have been an amateur student of some of these disciplines using reflections of my personal experiences. One can very well argue that it is very adventurous of anyone to try to attempt a topic so complex that many have failed to master. Well, my purpose of writing this book is not to put any definitive words on this, but to assimilate the multidisciplinary perspectives on this topic and logically highlight some of the points that I found interesting. This topic is quite tempting and all of us do think about it at some points in our lives. We get amazed by whatever we learn about our own selves. It is like an exploration of infinite space. Though we do not get all the answers, we do get fascinated by some of the explorations.

A genuine question could be—why this book? Well, I have read scores of books on the mind and brain. They are listed in the bibliography section. They are all good books, but they present a unidimensional view, be it science, artificial intelligence (AI), psychology, philosophy or religion. This topic needs a multidisciplinary approach to make any progress.

My attempt in this book has been to build a composite point of view based on the references from latest scientific studies in various universities, as well as ancient literature on this topic. To be honest, I have not been able to tie up all the loose ends. For that reason, it can only be an evolving book on an inscrutable topic. Having said that, I strongly believe that many of you will find the book interesting, educating and enriching, with many practical takeaways for your daily lives.

Acknowledgements

The topic of this book is tempting and inscrutable at the same time. A lot has been said about it already but still nothing is concrete and hence it leaves a lot of scope for exploration. The inspiration behind this book has been the writings of some of prominent authors of the past and current times. This topic required extensive research and hence I have read several books on this topic before creating a point of view. The reference to those authors is mentioned in the bibliographic section.

Writing a book is a long time-consuming process that requires constant motivation and encouragement. I thank my wife, Archana for allowing me to take frequent writing breaks to research as well as write on this topic. I thank my brother Anil Mishra for pointing me to various contents on this topic and for providing inputs on certain sections. I am also thankful to my friends and colleagues who have encouraged me to write and provided feedback on my writings.

I am grateful to Garuda Prakashan for selecting this book for publication. I thank Sankrant Sanu for providing guidance during the writing and editing process. He suggested me specifically to include the Indic perspectives as well on this topic. A lot has been said about Mind in ancient Vedic scriptures and other Indic writings. In the subsequent drafts, I tried to incorporate this missing aspect and I believe this has made the book more comprehensive. I am also thankful to Prashant Pandey for the constant guidance during the book publishing process. Finally, I thank my editor Anupama for helping me in the multiple rounds of the editing process and suggesting very important inputs.

Definition of 'Self'

*Tat tvam asi: Thou art That. Atman is Brahman: The Self in
each person is not different from the Godhead.*

—The Bhagavad Gita

*I*n the eighth century BC, an eight-year-old Adi
Shankara was asked by his guru, "Who are you?" He
replied in six verses known as 'Nirvana Shatakam'
which forms the basic teachings of Advaita Vedanta or
non-dualism. In the first five verses, he explains what he
is not. "I am not the mind, nor intellect, nor ego. I am not
the elements, nor the breath, nor the material. I have no
father, mother, friend or followers." He goes on to explain
further what he is not. In the last verse he says,

"aham nirvikalpo nirakara roopaha
vibhut vaacha sarvatra sarvendriyanam
na cha sangat naiva muktir na meyahh
chidananda rupa shivoham shivoham"

(I am without any attributes and form. I am present everywhere and behind all sense organs. I have no attachment to the world nor get liberated from anything. I am eternal bliss, I am Shiva.)

Just like Shankara, at some point in our lives, all of us are intrigued with what we call our own 'selves'. We are likely to ask–

> "Who am I? What makes me what I am?"
>
> "How do I relate to others? What is my place in this universe?"
>
> "Am I biologically more like animals or am I closer to the divine?"
>
> "Do I have a soul? Did I exist before? What will happen when I will die? Is my being just a brief spark surrounded by aeons of darkness on either side?"
>
> "Is human existence part of a grand design, an error or just a random occurrence? What is the purpose of our existence?"

We ask these questions to our individual self. The word 'individual' means something that can't be divided. This assumes our 'self' is one cohesive entity. However, our 'self' itself is a fractured aggregation. It is different with different people at different situations. There are little commonalities among these different identities we assume—a co-worker, a father, a husband, a neighbour or a close friend. We play different roles oblivious to each other with little overlap, as if we wear different masks in different situations. Even our behaviour may not be consistent in different roles— we can be a hard taskmaster, a caring husband, a jealous friend, and a demanding parent. However, there is still a common invisible narrative in all these roles that we play. This narrative is what we define as 'self'. This self is the common actor in all the situations it is faced with.

However, the real question is still unanswered— who sets the narrative for this self—is it our brain, mind or soul?

This seemingly innocuous question with very profound meaning has puzzled mankind since time immemorial and continues to baffle us even today. This process of inquiry has given birth to philosophies, religions, psychology and science. These questions are so deep that it has consumed generations of gurus, scientists and philosophers without any conclusive discovery. There are numerous hypotheses with little agreement, but the beauty of the human existence is that this enquiry continues, in all of us.

Let us compare our biology with those of other living beings. It may be worth noting that humans are not the most gifted living beings on this planet. We can hear sounds from 20Hz–20 kHz only. Dogs can hear up to 45 kHz, cats can hear up to 60 kHz and many other creatures can hear even more. They can also sense earthquakes much before humans can. The same goes for the visual abilities. Eagles can see more vividly than humans; they can even see ultraviolet light that humans can't detect. If we saw the colours the same way as eagles did, our world would look more brilliant. They have a navigation system aligned with the geostatic field that works like GPS—something that helps them fly thousands of kilometres during migration. They have a much better memory than humans. A bird remembers the exact location of its nest among the thousands of trees in a jungle. If you wonder why even the most modern police force still use dogs in investigations, you may be reminded that dogs have a sense of smell that is several thousand times stronger than that of humans. No technology has so far been able to replace the natural abilities of a dog's sense of smell. Similarly, there are animals that can run faster, jump higher and are physically far more powerful than us. In terms of pure biological supremacy, we are much below in the food chain on this planet. Nature has not bestowed humans with the best of physical and sensory abilities. We are not the most superior beings in that sense.

If you somehow believe that humans are the most intelligent species on this planet, hold that thought for a moment. A spider can spin a complex web that can beat the calculations of a bright mathematics PhD student. The student can write down Hooke's law on paper, but the spider understands it better and can apply that in practice to create the web that captures its prey by converting elastic potential energy into kinetic energy. Let us take other examples. Millions of ants can create an anthill in a purely synchronised way that we may not be able to comprehend at all. A flock of birds can fly in dynamic equilibrium, creating a beautiful formation with perfectly synchronised speed, direction and height. We may feel intelligent because we discovered Bernoulli's principle. However, nature provided the bird that insight much before our discovery of airplanes. A bat uses sonic waves and performs higher-order calculations to navigate through the surroundings that we may only feel astonished at. Our sophisticated brain can't even sense those signals, leave aside calculating distance from the objects at high speed. We can look for many examples where other living creatures are more intelligent and skilful than us. To sum it, nature has not bestowed humans with the best of mental faculties either. Intellectually, we are disadvantaged as well.

And yet, no animal has ever bothered with this question of self-definition. At least none of them have written any book or come forward to read the ones written by us. Why so? Because, the entire magic of animal kingdom is encoded in their biology, genes or what we may call nature. They function exactly as expected and in accordance with predefined natural laws. They can't break free from their biology. The same nature that has made them gifted physically and mentally, also made them biological captives of those abilities. Their biology is their destiny; they can never transcend it.

Humans on the other hand, have broken that barrier. We not only understand our biology and surroundings but have also started controlling them. We have grown beyond the encoded biological rules of evolution. Our biology is less important now. Our body is subservient to another organ called 'mind'. The day we started walking erect, our heads declared victory over the rest of our body, and our mind won over all other organs.

Why is the Process of Self-enquiry Unique to Humans?

This question has circular reasoning. Only humans worry about these questions and this process of inquiry makes them uniquely human. The famous quote by the French philosopher Rene Descartes, *Cogito, ergo sum* which is loosely translated as 'I think, therefore I am', captures it well. As a final argument on existence, he said that he could not doubt that he existed as he was the one who was doubting in the first place.

For thinking, we invented language. There is some hypothesis that thinking could happen using symbols and images as well, but language is the medium to communicate. This is the basis of cognitive revolution that sets us apart from other animals. No one knows at which point in time, humans stumbled upon this treasure in their brains or what triggered this. The development of the cognitive brain was the most important turning point in human history. This probably happened 10,000 years ago. What we call history, started from that point onwards. We set ourselves apart from animals. We started studying the animals and nature around us. We understood new rules and slowly started controlling them. Now in the 21st century, we can fly to the moon, create skyscrapers, and put all the apes in a zoo. Even if we are not able to control nature completely, we understand most of the underlying rules.

Let us come back to the question of self-enquiry. We feel completely at a loss when our own cognitive power turns itself on the brain that powers it. In a way, this creates a unique situation as no other organ in the human body can study itself—a heart does not try to argue with itself, a lever does not question its own functioning nor does an eye try to find out how vision works. But our mind can turn on itself. In the mathematical sense, this is a circular argument. We have a unique sense of reflection and observation— we can talk and watch ourselves talking. When we are making a presentation on a stage, our mind is focused on the act; at the same time, a part of our mind is also observing how we are performing. We act and evaluate our acting like a third person, at the same time.

All the homo sapiens can be traced back to a common gene pool, to the first inhabitants in Africa. More than 90 per cent of our genes, maybe a rough estimate of 97–99 per cent are common. So, biologically we are pretty much similar. Except for a little variation in colour, height or weight, we are almost like each other. Even our behaviour is the same; we cry in the same manner; we laugh in the same way and walk alike. Despite being so similar in physical attributes, we are completely different personalities. We can say that only our minds can account for this difference. Our cognitive power has large variance even though the underlying physical architecture of the brain is the same. If we can call our body the hardware and mind the software, we can safely say that though all of us have the same hardware, our software has vastly different versions. Our mind makes us different individuals.

So, a mind questions—does the mind exist?

This throws up unexpected outcomes ranging from complete denial to universal acceptance. This question can be so unsettling that even several lifetimes are not enough to find the answer. However, the process of enquiry continues—in each one of us, probably each passing day.

This imbroglio can be emulated in a practical experiment. Just ask anyone to describe himself as to who he is and observe the struggle he goes through.

He or she may define himself or herself in relation to someone like 'I am son of so and so, wife of so and so', etc. This is again a relative identity which has no meaning since the reference itself has no identity. This is like describing one link in the chain by pointing out other neighbouring links. Alternatively, the person can answer by saying in which profession he or she is working—'I am a doctor or an advocate', but this is again a very transient and superficial response. If I choose a profession, I do not become the profession. There is a constant struggle to find a constant element that we can call our intrinsic identity. Incidentally, the more we search for it, the more it deludes us.

In order to address this question, we can approach it from three different disciplines—theology, philosophy and neuroscience.

Vedic scriptures describe the mind at four different levels:

1. *Mann* (outer mind)—this creates the thoughts, feelings, desires, likes and dislikes.

2. *Buddhi* (intellect)—This is the conscious mind that analyses and decides based on the context. It can choose between right or wrong actions.

3. *Chitta* (subconscious mind)—It stores all the memories and subtle emotions that are repressed. We are not consciously aware of this.

4. *Ahankar* (Ego)—This creates our sense of identity around what we are and what we do. This also creates pride.

The above four are interlinked with each other and can manifest in different ways. The mind is combined existence of all the four components. Together, they are called *antah-karana*. The Vedas also state that the mind is a component of *maya* (illusion) that has been created by God, just as this universe. We are exceptional, thanks to God. So, to understand our mind, we need to understand God and his grand design of the universe.

When Hammurabi in ancient Babylon created the written code, he said that God had passed to him rules for society for the larger good of humanity. This was not a believable story, but it worked for the community at large and helped derive greater cooperation. The theological explanation was not open to questioning. Still, the human quest of enquiry could not be satiated forever. The theological explanation also raised several other questions—e.g., whether there was only one god or many gods. If God created everything by design, why there were so many famines and destruction? The moral concept of good versus evil was not able to explain the idea of an external god. A true seeking mind was never convinced with an entirely religious definition.

Even though the theologists could not provide an all-accepted answer to the existential question, they were aware of the enormity of the problem. In ancient India, there were two approaches to acquire knowledge—study of the universe or study of the self. It was believed that the human mind is as complex as the vast universe. A further quest to this also led to an alternative explanation that our mind is a macrocosm of the universe.

Now we know that there are a 100 billion neurons in our brain and there are roughly a same number of stars in our 'Milky Way' galaxy. This is beautifully captured in a poem by Emily Dickinson:

> *The Brain—is wider than the Sky—*
> *For—put them side by side—*
> *The one the other will contain*
> *With ease—and you—beside—*

One of the first principles and central essence of the Vedas is captured as—*Aham Bramhasmi* (I am the divine). This stated that the creator can't be separated from creation. If there was a god, it was in each one of us. It led to a stage where God and humans merged, and the quest of the identity pointed to the self again. It becomes a circular argument again—'to understand our self, one has to understand God, and to understand God, one has to understand the self'.

To bring some clarity, the Vedic scriptures described the self at five levels. The body that one gets is essentially created from food—it is called *Annamaya*. This creates all the physical parts and organs that we know of. Behind this food body, there is another self, consisting of vital breath. It is called *Pranamaya*. That is why ancient sages paid special attention to breathing techniques in the form of Yoga. Behind this layer, there is another self, consisting of will—called *Manomaya*. The next layer consists of consciousness which is called *Vigyanamaya atman*. The innermost layer of self is the pure bliss called *Anandamaya atman*.

The Upanishads describe human existence with an analogy of a chariot that has five horses. The horses have reins that are held by the charioteer and a passenger is sitting at the back. In this analogy, the chariot is the body, the horses are the five senses, the reins are the mind, the charioteer is the intellect and the passenger seated behind is the soul. It goes on to explain that ideally, the passenger should give directions to the charioteer who should pull the reins to guide the horses in the right direction. In essence, the soul should control the intellect, and the intellect should control the mind that should finally control the senses. Bhagavad Gita suggests that while our body is destructible, the 'inner self' or *atman* never dies, it just changes bodies like we change clothes. When Arjuna in Kurukshetra says that he doesn't want to kill his own kith and kin, Shri Krishna tells him the soul is indestructible anyway.

ya enaṁ vetti hantāraṁ yaśh chainaṁ manyate hatam
ubhau tau na vijānīto, nāyaṁ hanti na hanyate

(Whosoever thinks that the soul can slay or can be slain, they are ignorant. A soul can never kill, and it can't be killed either.)

The second most audacious attempt to understand 'who we are' has been from philosophy. It does not ascribe everything to the supreme authority of God but rather to our sense of reasoning. However, it still can't be proven by experimentation. One of the notable works in this field was done by the French philosopher Rene Descartes. He subdivided the 'self' further into mind–body dualism. According to him, the mind and body both operate in different domains. The body deals with the physical aspects and can be measured objectively, and the mind has an element of subjectivity or 'qualia' that can't be defined precisely.

However, there was a problem in this dualist theory as well—how do the mind and body coordinate with each other if they operate in completely different domains and do not understand each other's languages? This was an even more baffling question for which Descartes struggled to provide an answer. He theorised that they talk to each other through a special organ called pineal gland where all our thoughts reside. He regarded this as the principal seat of the soul. With more detailed study of the human brain, however, it became clear that there was no mysticism in this organ, and it was no different from other parts of the body. The basis of soul fell flat once again and the question of 'who are we' remained as intriguing as ever.

One of the unique aspects of humans is their unique personality. Though we all look similar (well almost), we think, believe and act differently. Some are intelligent while some are not so bright (at least some people think that way), some could be introverts, some could be extroverts, some are aggressive while some are calm. The spectrum is so wide that every person can be uniquely defined without any overlap. This uniqueness of the personality was attributed to the soul or mind. It was presumed that the mind does not have any physical equivalence like brain, and they are different. Our characters can't be mapped to brain architecture, scientists believed.

An incident in 1848, however, challenged this perspective.

> *Phineas Gage was an American railroad worker in Vermont. A part of his job required him to use explosives to break the rocks and make way for laying the rails. One fine day, while he was packing the rock hole with gunpowder and was cramming it in, suddenly the fuse misfired. The impact of the explosion was so huge that the tamping iron rod in his hand pierced through his lower jaw on the left side and passed through his*

skull, taking off part of his brain with it. Imagine a crowbar 43 inches long and weighing 13 pounds passing through the skull of a human. Most probably he would have died, and remember it was 1848 when there was not specialised medical care.

However, somehow Phineas Gage survived. He subsequently became one of the most studied patients in neuroscience, not because of his head injury, but because of the apparent change in his personality. Before the accident, he was a very amicable and friendly person, but after the accident he became very aggressive and irritable. Even his planning and execution skills that were exemplary earlier suffered a great deal, and he could not keep his job. He lived 12 years after the accident.

The above incident proved that personality or character was somewhat linked with brain function and it doesn't have any independent existence. Scientifically, it also debunked the theory of the soul. Neuroscientists claimed that our personality is all governed by the tiny brain cells called neurons, just that they are too complex to fully understand now. This accident also proved that our brain is highly resilient and can handle self-recovery in a remarkable way. Imagine an iron bar piercing through the hard disk of even the most advanced computer. There is no way the computer would function after that.

Before we try further to understand the approach of medical science, it is important to draw a difference between the brain and the mind. The brain is the physical structure consisting of neurons housed inside our skulls. The mind on the other hand is an abstract concept that does not have any physical equivalence, or so it seems. In fact, for theology and philosophy, this was a not a problem, as the concept of mind (and soul) helped them in explaining the uniqueness of humans. The concept of good and bad was ingrained in the soul. The mind was like a naughty child under the supervision of the soul. The concept of soul was a powerful tool for religious leaders, even though it could never be directly observed.

Though science has not denied the existence of the mind, their primary area of interest has been the functioning of the brain.

The field of neuroscience for a long time refused to accept the genuine enquiry of the existential self as a problem statement. The study of consciousness was a waste of time, because science which relied on the phenomenon of measurement had no way to measure the subjective experiences of different people. While they denied the existence of soul, the neuroscientists could not explain the existence of mind. The mind according to them, was nothing real but an emergent property of the brain when millions of neurons fired electrochemical signals in a certain way. They tried to explain the concept of self as an interaction pattern of the neural signals. The brain creates the illusion of mind—they explained. It is like the traffic in a busy city. If we study the movement of a single car, we will fail to understand traffic jams in the city. Only when we study the movements of all the cars together at the same time, we would be able to understand traffic. So, traffic is an emergent property of millions of cars moving in the city. Similarly, human brains have billions of neurons and the myriads of electrical patterns in them give rise to the mind. Since we don't have enough processing power to simulate these billions of neuronal electrical activities, we can't simulate the mind. Every thought can be explained in terms of physical activities in the brain. But this is again a very reductionist approach and does not go too far in explaining why such a unique concept of mind appears only for humans and no other mammals.

At every neuron level, we have a pretty good understanding, biologically. It was earlier believed that the human brain is a one huge, gigantic network unlike the other cells in the body. However, the discovery of the electron microscope proved that the neurons are small cells that are interconnected at synapses. Each cell consists of many dendrites (receptors of electric impulses and chemical signals) that aggregate at the cell body called soma. This connects to the long tail called axon that virtually acts like a transmission wire to reach the other end before connecting to the dendrites of other neurons. Some axons are myelinated to preserve the electrochemical signals over a distance.

This all seems straightforward at the individual neuron level. Brain scientists today understand this very well. What they don't understand is the 'network effect' of these neurons. When billions of them interact, they give rise to something called emergent property. It is like at each molecule level, water, vapour and ice are all the same, but their network effect is entirely different. If we try to study the 'wetness' by looking at each water molecule, we will fail to understand it; it must be studied in aggregate; it has collective existence.

But Why We Cannot Study the Collective or Aggregate?

In data science it is called 'curse of dimensionality'. As we increase the number of elements, their interaction multiplies exponentially so much that they become incomputable soon. At such levels, interactions become so significant that individual elements lose their properties or become immaterial. The collective is not the sum of elements—they are non-linear. So, one can't understand the collective by studying the elements. We will have to study the aggregate as a whole. We can't study the country by studying the inhabitants, and we can't understand the anthills by knowing how the individual ant works. The same complexity applies for the genes. We have sequenced the human genome. We know the individual genes, but they hardly have been helpful in predicting future diseases. In rare cases where a single gene is responsible for a disease, we can make some predictions. But most of the disease behaviour is governed by the interactions of different genes. These interactions are mathematically complex or incomputable.

Study of the human brain is one of the most humbling experiences for those who think science has made big advancements already. Sigmund Freud, the noted psychologist first started as a neurologist. He was a doctor of medicine and an expert in neuropathology in Austria, way back in 1881. However, he did realise that our scientific understanding of the human brain would take several centuries. He rather chose the path of psychoanalysis which became quite prevalent later as a tool of understanding human behaviour. Even today, our understanding of the human mind is at best, primitive.

Our current level of understanding of the brain is akin to learning the alphabets, but we still don't understand the language of the brain. Alphabets are only the first step to learn the language, then there are words, grammar and semantics. We are quite far from reaching those milestones. Some are doubtful if we will ever be able to reach there. But there is some hope that with increasing computing power and rise of artificial intelligence, we can unravel the language of the brain. We will have to redefine what it means to be a human in that era.

As of now, it is very clear that all the three disciplines of knowledge seekers are at the same starting point when it comes to applying our mind on ourselves—to understand who we are. With SpaceX programme from Elon Musk, some of us can hopefully reach Mars one day. However, there is lesser hope that we will be able to turn our intellect inward to fully understand who we are. Our relative existence in this world does not lead to any conclusions either. This makes this self-inquiry problem the most interesting one, humans have faced ever.

> "The most terrifying fact about the universe is not that it is hostile but that it is indifferent, but if we can come to terms with this indifference, then our existence as a species can have genuine meaning. However vast the darkness, we must supply our own light."

The above quote by Stanley Kubrick captures the human's relation with the universe very well. Our process of enquiry is central to our existence. The universe is meaningless; it is our enquiry that gives meaning to it.

The metaphor of Indra's net describes this self in Atharva Veda. According to it, Indra's net is an infinitely expansive net extended in all directions. At each crossing point of the net, is a jewel. Each jewel is reflected in all the other jewels. Each jewel is intimately connected with all other jewels and any change in even a single jewel effects the reflection. Jewels in this metaphor are the individuals. Indra's net depicts the oneness of the universe and the interconnectedness of everything. It means that the self can't exist without the whole and there is no whole without the self. Incidentally, contemporary physicists agree that this is a good metaphor of the universe and our existence in it.

Key takeaways from our attempts of self-enquiry:

1. We as thinking beings, always wonder about our existence with questions like—who we are, what is the purpose of our existence, and how are we different from other living beings.

2. Though we may think we are exceptional, nature has not bestowed us with the best of physical or mental abilities. Animals are

sometimes more intelligent and skilful than humans, but their intelligence is encoded in their biology. They can't change that in their lifetime. Humans are the only fortunate species who have broken free from their biology.

3. When we think of who we are—three different but related concepts come to the picture—soul, mind and brain. Religion or spirituality deals with the idea of soul, psychology and philosophy explains the mind, while medical science goes entirely with the concept of brain.

4. Though there is no scientific proof for the soul, one can't deny the existence of the mind. The main challenge the mind poses—it is subjective and can't be studied empirically.

5. Early philosophers proposed that the mind and body work in completely different domains. While the body deals with the material property, the mind does not follow any material law. This was known as the dualist theory proposed by Rene Descartes.

6. Our personality is not defined by the soul but by the structure of our brain. Change or damage to our brain can change our personality as seen in the case of Phineas

Gage, the crowbar operator who became aggressive after brain damage.

7. From the perspective of medical science, we have a pretty good understanding of how the individual neurons of our brain work. An adult has close to 100 billion neurons with each neuron having up to 10,000 connections. This creates up to a quadrillion connections in the human brain.

8. Though we understand the functioning of individual neurons, we don't know how they behave as a network. It is like trying to understand the economy of a country by studying the activities of the individuals.

9. The mind is an emergent property that results from the activities of the brain. Though medical science can't yet prove it, neuroscientists can't deny its existence.

10. Despite current advancements in science, we are still at an infancy when it comes to neuroscience. With the rise of computing power and artificial intelligence, we may have a better chance of unravelling the brain in the future.

Search for Happiness

Happiness is not something ready-made. It comes from your own actions.

—Dalai Lama

A US scientist once bought a South American lizard and brought it home as a pet. The pet owner noticed that the lizard stopped eating since it was brought to its new home in the United States. Since it was a new environment for the lizard, the pet owner thought it was a temporary problem and the lizard would adjust to it with time. He brought all kinds of food, but the lizard would just refuse to eat. He killed flies and presented them to the lizard, but it did not eat. He offered it rice and bread. He offered it meat but to no avail. In the meantime, the lizard was growing weak. The owner thought that the lizard would die of starvation.

One day, he offered the lizard ham and bread. When the lizard refused to eat that, the scientist covered it with a newspaper and left it on the table. To his surprise, the lizard suddenly moved into action, shredded the newspaper, and ate the bread. On further analysis, the scientist realised that the basic nature of the lizard is hunting for food, and shredding things before eating.

This is how happiness works in humans as well. It results from the pursuit of a challenging goal. If the outcome is given on a platter, it may not result in the same level of happiness. This seems counter-intuitive but is true if we analyse carefully.

I recall a friend of mine who often repeated words like 'I want to be happy'. Ironically, he used to be often upset with something or the other and repeated those words in anxiety. It became annoying for all of us beyond a point. To stop him from repeating those words, we used to pre-empt him when he would say 'I want to be happy'. We nicknamed him 'Mr Happy' though he was unhappy most of the time. We used to make fun of him time and again for being so childish.

On second thought, my friend was no different from each one of us who have the same quest, just that he articulated it explicitly. He was more honest with his feelings. We all chase happiness. All through our lives, we keep asking this question—'what would make us happy'. We keep following the shifting goal posts—when we are in school, we think that going to college will make us happy; when we join college, then we think of a job and so on and so forth. The chase never stops. This perennial chase also exhausts us at times, and we get intrigued by our own search for happiness. Most of us believe that the purpose of human life is essentially to be happy.

Sigmund Freud's main argument was that human beings are hedonistic. They search for happiness in everything they do. We also know that happiness has no well-defined formula. That is why we keep chasing it, be it a holiday in a foreign location or buying a car.

But Why is Happiness Important in Human Life?

Search for happiness may have some evolutionary basis. A happy person has higher chances of survival. If you are in some physical pain or suffering, it affects your well-being and happiness. We work towards getting rid of it—hence, good for our survival. A healthy and fit body is good for us, but we pretty much know that the search for happiness is well beyond physical well-being, it is a lot more psychological.

If you get a salary hike of 20 per cent in your job, you feel happy. For a few moments, you feel at the top of the world. Money brings happiness, you feel. Happiness seems no longer elusive—you believe you finally cracked the formula. Then you meet your friends at the lunch table and get to know that three of them got a 30 per cent hike and yours was the lowest among them. Your happiness evaporates in no time—it turns into grief. You suddenly feel miserable and awful. You recall that last year, though your hike was just 10 per cent, it was the highest among your friends. You were at the top of the world. Even though it is twice as big a hike this time, it has made you sad and angry instead.

Similarly, if you fail in a test, you feel horrible but if you get to know that none of your friends have passed, your sadness somehow wears off. You think your relative position is not affected in any way. So even a million-dollar salary is no guarantee for happiness. What matters is how much your friends are earning.

The above situation is weird and irrational in a way, but it is so true. Our mental state of happiness does not depend on absolute benefits but how well or badly we are doing compared to our peers who act as reference points. Happiness it appears, is relative. So, if you were alone on this planet and there were no one to compare with, you would never be happy.

Why our Brain Defines Success not in Absolute Terms but Relative Terms?

One theory says that the brain does this comparison because it does not know what is good in absolute terms. For the brain confined in the darkness of our cranium, there is very little to know if a particular outcome is the best possible outcome. So, it uses comparison as the tool. If someone else has achieved a better outcome, then your current outcome is labelled suboptimal, and it triggers the unhappiness circuit. This has some evolutionary benefits, as it ensures that everyone strives for the best outcome possible. This ensured the collective well-being of the tribes in the hunter-gatherer days. It is ironical, however, that the same comparison tool that was meant for ensuring our well-being makes us miserable instead.

Another thing about happiness is, it has strong negativity bias. If the share market goes up 10 per cent one day and goes down by the same 10 per cent the next day, technically your wealth is the same as it was two days back. But your mind sees it differently. While a 10 per cent rise generates x level of happiness, the 10 per cent fall generates much more than x level of unhappiness. Eventually, it makes us more unhappy than happy for the same level of opposite change. Daniel Kahneman calls this, the 'prospect theory or loss-aversion theory'. He postulates that our mind acts irrationally in this case. As per his research, the pain from losing 1,000 dollars could only be compensated by a gain of 2,000 dollars. This is a very significant theory in behavioural science for which Daniel Kahneman also received the Noble Prize.

Happiness is the most researched area by philosophers, psychologists and theologists. They all disagree on what drives happiness, but they all agree that it has a very intrinsic value in human lives. There has been so much interest in this field from psychologists that there is a new branch of psychology dedicated to it—positive psychology. The purpose of positive psychology is not to treat mentally ill people but to make less happy people happier. This is to research what makes our life worth living for.

For better understanding, happiness could be defined at three levels.

When you eat some good food, watch a good movie, or get a good salary hike, you feel happy about it. It can be physical, emotional or even symbolic. But you definitely feel a sense of happiness. You can call it pleasure. We all seek pleasure in our day-to-day lives. But Aristotle did not consider this pleasure as real happiness, something that you may get from great contemplation or having an intellectually intense discussion with a friend. Even in the ancient Indian value system, pleasure is something that is looked down upon. The wise sages always spurned this form of happiness because they believed it is very short-lived.

In ancient Indian philosophy, this corresponds to the *Charvakas* school of thoughts. The *Charvakas* did not believe in the Vedas or God. Their main argument was that the main objective of life is to eat, drink and be happy. There is nothing beyond the material world that we can't perceive through our senses. There is no point of 'good *karma*' because this is the only life we have, and we must take maximum advantage of this. They focused on material pleasure. Vedas on the other hand talk about *shreyas* and *preyas*. *Preyas* appear pleasant to the senses but they harm us in the long run. *Shreyas* on the other hand may be unpleasant or even painful in the short term but will help greatly in the long run. Tasty junk food versus healthy food is an example of the same. The wise people select *shreyas* over *preyas* for long-term happiness.

The pleasure-driven happiness, the first form of happiness, has a weird characteristic—it always seeks novelty. It is not possible to be in a sustained state of happiness using this form. Any familiarity quickly turns into boredom. This can explain why rich and wealthy people may also face bouts of sadness.

The second form of happiness is what comes from flow. We all have experienced this. When an artist is engrossed in a painting or a programmer is working on code—this is a state of flow. Here the mind is so engrossed in work that we lose the sense of time and space. Our attention is fully concentrated on the work at hand. We have no more attention left to attend to anything else around us. The time flies like anything. In this state, we also sometimes forget to eat or drink, but we don't mind. We feel happy about it even though it may exhaust us at times. In the book *Ikigai: A Japanese Secret to a Long and Happy Life*, the authors define happiness as the act of being busy. The long-lived citizens of the island of Okinawa village were continuously in a state of 'flow' working in their vegetable fields, cooking, dancing and singing.

Paul S Kalanithi, in his book, *When Breath Becomes Air* talks about his experience as a neurosurgeon in the operation theatre: "It seemed to me that the wall clocks had hands at two arbitrary positions." He used to be so engrossed in surgery that he never experienced the elapse of time. Abraham Maslow called this as 'peak experience'. This is the reason some people love their profession because the flow makes them happy. Flow- driven happiness is more lasting than pleasure-driven happiness.

The third form of happiness is when we strive for the purpose or larger meaning of our lives. What makes our lives worth living? Why do we go through the daily grind of ups and downs? Is there a purpose behind that, given that we are all dead in the long term?

Physicist Michio Kaku in his book *The God Equation* mentions that all his life, the noted Einstein was in search of one single equation that could explain the theory of everything. Einstein's secretary, Helen Dukas, once mentioned that he received overwhelming letters pleading with him to explain the meaning of life and asking if he believed in God. Einstein said he was helpless to answer these questions about the purpose of life and the universe. Though he did not believe in a personal God—one who rewards the believers and punishes the non-believers, he did believe in the cosmic God—the one that has made this world beautiful, elegant, and simple. He was enamoured by the order and the grand design of our universe, and hence it was meaningful from that perspective.

When philosophers talk of happiness, they refer to finding this meaning in our lives. This is the most lasting form of happiness. Incidentally, it does not have a universal answer. The meaning can be different for every person. Probably people find meaning beyond the self, by connecting with other people, communities or countries. When you feel that you are a part of the larger design of the universe and you have a role to play, you have found meaning. You conclude that you are not a random occurrence.

In the book *Until the End of Time,* the author Brian Greene, a professor of physics and mathematics talks of a thought experiment with his audience in a conference. He described two scenarios—in the first scenario, imagine you get to know that you will die in a year, and in the second, imagine you get to know that the whole world will come to an end in a year. In both the cases, you die in a year but there is a fundamental difference between the two. While the first scenario motivates us to act, the second scenario makes it appear as though all the actions are pointless. What is the point of going to school, writing a book, or doing some research when everything will end? We know we are mortals, but we also have a quest for immortality through our actions. We believe someone will carry on from where we left, even when we die. We get a sense of continuity. This gives us some meaning for what we do.

Victor Frankl in his book *Man's Search for Meaning,* says we generally associate happiness with pleasure, health, wealth, etc., and people with these things have higher chances of survival. But people can even survive terrible adversaries and tragedies if they can see some larger purpose in that suffering.

The book captures stories of people in the concentration camp in Auschwitz and how they try to make sense of the atrocities committed on them.

Victor Frankl, a psychiatrist, and a prison inhabitant himself, describes the day-to-day struggle of the inmates from close quarters. Every day, the old and sick were being sent to gas chambers; those in the camp were forced into work all day long without food and medicines. They were separated from their families and always wondered if their loved ones were alive or sent to gas chambers already. There was no way to communicate with the outside world. The probability of coming out alive from the camp was very remote, as there was no end date of prison terms.

The author says under these most inhuman conditions, people died in large numbers every day. He points out that the first among those who died were not the weakest ones but the ones who lost hope for the future and could not find a meaning to their predicament. Those who had found some purpose had a greater chance of survival in the camp. The author says he survived because he wanted to complete a manuscript upon his release from the camp. This sense of purpose kept him alive. Victor felt so strongly about this subject that he evolved a new field of research called 'logotherapy—therapeutic science of finding meaning in life'.

This is not only true for people in concentration camps but for everyone in life—a sense of meaning is most crucial for human existence. The aim of human life is not momentary pleasure but hope for their future. Even the suffering does not matter; people happily endure suffering if they find some meaning in it.

If meaning is so important for our existence, what is the answer so far? Many philosophers have said that the universe is meaningless, it has no purpose.

As Victor Frankl in his book says, "There is no universal answer—it varies from man to man and moment to moment, but there is always a meaning that we have to look for." He compares this to a game of chess. A chess grandmaster can't answer what is the best chess move in a generic way—it depends on the context of the play and opposition. Different chess positions have very different answers for the best possible move.

Similarly, every human life and the context are unique as they can't be replicated or repeated. As soon as one realises that he or she is irreplaceable because only he or she can achieve the objectives, the existential vacuum disappears. This act of finding that meaning is a healthy tension when one finds the gap between the current state and the aspirational state. Lack of that tension can result in boredom that is killing more people today than distress.

Most of us assign meaning to our lives by the work we do, however futile that may be. We feel that we are contributing to society in some way, we are relevant for others. We find meaning in that relevance. Once we retire from active work, we lose that anchor. This is the reason that retirement is considered a difficult life stage to deal with.

Raising a child is full of difficult times. A toddler can put even a patient person to test. It is a very stressful activity. But if the parents see the larger meaning in the activity, their momentary stress does not matter. Similarly, teaching could be a good way to find meaning. Serving your community, religion or country could be another conduit to find meaning. A wounded soldier in pain still thinks that his life is worth living. Martyrdom is invariably eulogised in all cultures because people find happiness in serving their country. In all these situations, happiness is an indirect outcome of an activity we consider meaningful. This is the golden rule—any direct pursuit of happiness is almost certain to fail.

Unfortunately for some, the meaning of life may not adhere to a moral code. A terrorist who is brainwashed with a dangerous ideology and goes on to commit a grievous crime, might feel equally happy. Killing a fellow human being is bad but when they believe they are doing that for a larger cause, they find meaning in the act. They believe their life is worth the cause, even when others condemn their horrible acts. The purpose can be misleading as well, as in this case.

Sometimes, we think of happiness as adding things to our lives—buying a car, a house or a diamond ring. The reductionist theory claims the contrary—you can be happier by reducing things from your life. Wealth, for example, brings with it its own share of anxiety. Success brings its own share of vulnerability. According to this theory, having a minimalist approach in life can be more rewarding from the happiness perspective. This was practiced by monks in ancient times, who relinquished all material belongings in search of absolute happiness. The Vedic literature describes attachment as the main reason for our unhappiness. Attachment creates desire for specific outcomes with events and people. If that does not happen, we get angry and sad. But, even when we can fulfil our desires, but it does not satiate the same, it creates greed to get more of them. It is a vicious cycle that is triggered by material attachment. This is captured well in the following verse from Kabir:

maya mui na man muva, mari mari gaya sareer
aasa trishna na mui, yon kahi gaya Kabir

(Even when the body perishes many times, the mind and desire never vanish. The materialistic desire never dies, says Kabir.)

The Vedic scriptures also say that attachment is the constant thought about something, and it is inevitable for the mind. The mind can't be stopped from thinking, so attachment is unavoidable. The only solution is to focus the mind on higher and noble causes including spiritual attachment. Buddha also looked at the world in the similar way—"There is misery in the world. Misery has a cause. The cause of the misery is desire. If the desire is eradicated, misery will be eradicated."

One of the things that goes counter to happiness is worry. Worry creates anxiety and makes us unhappy. In his book *Life's Amazing Secrets*, Gaur Gopal Das explains this with a very simple but powerful flowchart. Do you have a problem? No—then why worry? If yes—then the question you need to ask is, can you do something about it? If no—then why worry? If yes— then, do the things in your control. If you can do things in your control, there should not be any worry. The end action for all the pathways is 'why worry'. The key conclusion is that we need to detach ourselves from the uncontrollable outcomes and there will not be any need to worry. Most of the times we get mixed up between the controllable and uncontrollable things that cloud our judgements, and this makes us worried. We worry about things that are beyond us while ignoring the bit that is within our own control.

Neuroscientists look at happiness as a special state of brain which is more like experiencing the sensation of pleasure. Scientist have discovered that the incidents by themselves do not provide happiness, but it is our biochemical reaction to the events that gives us happiness. The specific actions of the neurons are rewarded by the flow of a neurotransmitter called dopamine. This is how the brain learns a desirable behaviour—more dopamine indicates it is a pleasurable experience and the brain strengthens that behaviour. Less flow of dopamine indicates that the behaviour need not be learnt. This is called the reinforcement theory of brain learning.

> There was an experiment done on rats to understand how the pleasure circuit operates in the brain. The rats were fitted with electrodes that could electrically stimulate the part of the brain that releases dopamine. They were provided with a mechanical lever that when pulled, activated the electrodes. The rats eventually pulled the levers repeatedly to the extent of starving themselves. So, the flow of dopamine can even overcome the basic biological needs like hunger.

For a long time, I wondered why people like long-distance running. It makes the body tired and exhausted—leave aside the professional athletes but why anyone would ever do that for fun? Is there any fun in exhausting ourselves? However, once I took up running, grudgingly, I had a completely different experience. Although my body and legs were in pain, my brain was emitting positive signals after just a few minutes of an hour-long run. It was a kind of happy feeling. Now I understand why people get so hooked on to running marathons. I read about it later—it is called 'runner's high'. This results in a state of euphoria coupled with reduced anxiety and less ability to feel pain. This comes from endorphins that are released by our brain during running.

The reason why this 'happiness circuit' is triggered during running might again have some evolutionary reasons. For our hunter-gatherer forefathers, running was crucial to finding food and protecting themselves from being hunted. So, despite sore legs and tired bodies, running has a good value in providing happiness. If you want a short cut to being happy—try running. It is not only beneficial for physical well-being but mental well-being as well.

Search for Happiness Tablets

Our brain does not know the external world; it only reacts to the flow of hormones like endorphins and dopamine that make us feel happy. So, if we can somehow control the flow of these hormones, we can achieve this evasive happiness without doing anything else. Today, some drugs are already being used to treat depression. Addictive drugs like cocaine also work like that, producing short-term euphoria.

As medical science progresses further, the day is not far off when we can all take a tablet to feel happy. However, this will be only true for the first level of happiness—pleasure. Its effect will be momentary till the hormones remain active. The task of finding the higher order of happiness like finding meaning in life can still not be solved by any tablet. Till such time, we will have to look up to the psychologists and philosophers to help us find our place in this universe.

American anthropologist Ernest Becker writes about our existential dilemma:

"We are under a constant existential tension, pulled towards the sky by a consciousness that can soar to the heights of Shakespeare, Beethoven and Einstein but tethered to Earth by a physical form that will decay to dust. Man is literally split into two: he has an awareness of his own splendid uniqueness in that he sticks out of nature with towering majesty, and yet he goes back into the ground a few feet in order blindly and dumbly to rot and disappear forever."

During medieval times and earlier when man asked the question—who he is and what is his purpose in life, someone told him that God has created this universe and made us the central subject on Earth. He has done the grand design of the world and provided us with a set of rulebooks on how to lead our lives. There are rewards for living our lives in the prescribed way and punishments when we deviate from them. Man was convinced with the story of religion and it somehow satiated his quest on the 'why' and 'how'. Life became meaningful to him.

But soon enough, man got to know that Earth was not at the centre of the universe. This giant Earth itself was just a tiny speck among the innumerable planets, stars and galaxies. These heavenly bodies were held together by gravitation in the vast universe. In fact, the entropy (disorderliness) of the universe is only increasing every moment and every ordered thing including life is naturally inclined to decay. There was no grand design and most of the things in the universe are dark and inhospitable. The man is not the hero in the story of the universe. He is not even a sub-plot. He is one of the several accidental things that are inconsequential in the larger scheme of things.

Life from this perspective lacks any meaning. Every waking day, we pin our hopes on tomorrow.

But every tomorrow brings us closer to our death. For all the praiseworthy acts and grand thoughts, we slowly decay and one day just vanish. Our momentary life is a brief spark in the darkness of eternity on either side of the life event. Death cleans up our existence completely and we remain no more than a link in the long survival chain. We, and nothing in us is permanent. Therefore, William James said, "Knowledge of death is the worm at the core of all our usual springs of delight." In our everyday life, we pretend that death does not exist, but we very well know that eventual destruction awaits all of us and we can't escape that. This was the biggest dilemma for the existentialist philosophers.

What is the point of everyday suffering and pain when we know all this is going to be eventually wiped out from existence? Therefore Albert Camus, the famous French philosopher said that the only philosophical problem we all should urgently address is whether human lives are so absurd that suicide is the only solution. If nothing we do in this life lasts eventually, what is the point of living with this absurdity. In his book *Myth of Sisyphus*, he compares life with the condemned Greek god who was punished to roll a big boulder up a hill every day only to see it roll down the next morning. Life is that big boulder we try to push uphill, and our disillusionment continues. The author finally concludes that yes, life is absurd, but we should not commit suicide because we must revolt against this absurdity— by living positively and discovering the meaning in an otherwise meaningless world.

Key points for takeaway:

1. Our pursuit of life is pursuit of happiness in a way. Happiness has evolutionary basis. A happy person is expected to live longer and create healthy offspring.

2. The brain has no way to figure out what is the best outcome under a given context. It uses the tool of comparison with other human beings as a benchmark. That is the reason we get so affected by our relative position in our peer group.

3. There are three stages of happiness—pleasure, flow and meaning. Pleasure is the temporary happiness we get by eating good food or watching a good movie. Flow is something that we experience as an artist when we get absorbed while painting. The third stage is when we find a larger purpose in our lives.

4. When the philosophers talk of happiness, they never mean pleasure that is transient. The sensual pleasures are looked down upon

in search of higher-order happiness like purposeful lives.

5. If one finds the larger meaning in an activity, even a life of suffering is happily endured. Child-rearing for example, is a very stressful and draining activity but most parents happily go through that. Motivated people are happily willing to sacrifice everything, including their own lives.

6. A physical activity like running emits hormones that gives us a sensation of pleasure. Though it tires our body and generates physical pain, our brain sends positive signals that is sometimes called 'runner's high'.

7. Happiness results as an indirect outcome from the pursuit of a goal. If the outcome is given to us on a platter, we don't experience the same happiness that can result from striving for it. Any direct search for happiness is more likely to be a disappointment.

8. The self is a wrong place to search for happiness. It invariably results from activities that are larger than the self—be it family, community, religion or the country.

9. We pretty much understand the neurological aspects of pleasure-sensation in our brain.

The scientists have discovered the hormones responsible for making us happy. The day is not very far when we can buy 'happiness tablets' for the sensation of pleasure.

10. Though some medicines can provide us short-term pleasure, the long-term happiness will still be evasive. It is a personal quest for each of us individually.

Our Fallible Memory

Memory... is the diary that we all carry about with us.

—Oscar Wilde

Probably you may have seen a movie (especially the 80s movies from Bollywood) where the actor is driving a car on a hilly road, happily singing a song and enjoying his journey. Suddenly, his car skids at the sharp bend and there is a brake failure. The car slips through the precipice to fall several feet into the valley. Thankfully, the protagonist is saved miraculously by clinging onto a tree as the car goes for a free fall and finally catches fire after a loud blast. The falling car as a fireball creates a spectacular cinematography. For the movie, the story just begins there.

Soon, the spotlight comes back to the hero, still precariously hanging onto a small branch of the tree on the slope. It could break at any moment, but thankfully it does not. The audience is relieved that the actor survives through the terrible accident, but there is a twist (or is it predictable?). The hero has hurt himself in the head due to which he has lost his memory entirely. He can't even remember his name, or where he came from or anything about his past life. As a worse misfortune, he does not even carry any identity card, so no one has a clue of who he could be. He is a completely new person now. The village head allows him to stay with them till he recovers.

The new story unfolds until one day, the actor recovers his lost memory (possibly due to another accident at the same spot), but not before the daughter of the village head falls in love with him. By now his life is a mad mix of two disparate lives and he meticulously tries to juggle between the two. I know that the millennials today will reject a story like this outright— 'what about the biometrics and face recognition?' Ok—this storyline is from the 80s, and we did not have an Aadhaar card then. Now Bollywood has stopped making such movies because it is pure fantasy.

Hollywood is equally fascinated by memory-based movie plots. In the movie *Eternal Sunshine of the Spotless Mind,* two people accidentally meet each other in a train and they are attracted to each other immediately. Later, they discover that they had been lovers in the past and after a bad fight one day, they asked their memories to be erased completely. However, their emotions were intact and got triggered when they saw each other. In the movie *Men in Black,* the protagonist Will Smith uses a neutraliser to erase the inconvenient memories of alien encounters. Using a dial, he is also able to specify how much of memory he wants to erase. They also implant false memories in people's brains.

Plots like the ones mentioned above makes for an amusing storytelling, that the film makers have exploited quite well. In common parlance, it is called amnesia or selective amnesia. This also suggests how our identity is defined by our memory. The memory creates a thread of continuity to anchor our self in the fast-changing environment. When we lose our memory, we are a completely new person. If we are not able to form a new memory, we are a new person at every moment. Our constant self is lost. That is why it is so challenging for people suffering from dementia and Alzheimer's disease.

Early Learning and Memory Formation

As a child, I had a very peculiar way of learning. I could memorise my school textbook literally word for word and reproduce it verbally. I had a weird ritual for doing so; most often I would lie down on the bed, sometimes cover myself with the blanket, close my eyes, and speak aloud the lessons for several minutes, sometimes hours. If someone else would have seen me in that state, they would have concluded that I was sleep talking. It helped me tremendously in some subjects like geography, biology, social science, and literature. I could also use this method in subjects like mathematics and science.

The retrieval of memory during the exam was even trickier. Even though the questions were within the scope of the textbook, I would take a few minutes to recall which chapter, page and starting line, the answer corresponded to. The pages with words were stored as images in my brain. Once I knew the start, I was very quick to reproduce the answer without any error. Though this way of learning reduced with time, some aspects of this habit continued even during my college.

All of us are familiar with this method of learning by memorising things. This methodology can be called 'Rote Learning'—a clear 'no' in modern times. Good schools encourage students to ask questions and not memorise things that are taught to them. We often see advertisements from elite schools —'we give personalised attention to students to nurture their creative talent and discourage memory-based learning' (of course, for a very exorbitant fee that is mentioned in fine print).

Is Memory-Intensive Learning Bad?

The ancient Indian education system was possibly based on this where the teachers passed on the knowledge in a *gurukul* type of setup. They would recite Sanskrit *shlokas* and repeat with their teachers (first just rhyming without knowing the meaning of it and later reflecting on the meaning as part of meditation). Most of the Vedic knowledge was transferred orally; there are very little written records. Possibly during the early period of the Vedas, writing was not even invented. The original Vedas are called *Shruti* (something that has been heard) and other Vedic literature are known as *Smriti* (something that has been recalled from memory). There are thousands of hymns in the Vedas that the scholars memorised collectively and passed on from one generation to another over several centuries. It required 10–20 years of dedicated study, but it was humanly possible to memorise all those hymns. Even when writing was discovered, the Vedic scholars desisted from writing the oral knowledge because they thought it was almost sacrilegious to write them on paper. The point that I want to make is that human memory can be exploited to great limits if used properly.

Even during our school days, studying Sanskrit used to be fun for that reason—it was so easy to memorise rhyming *shlokas*. Ascribing the meaning later was quite easy. If we observe the language skills of infants, they also exhibit a similar pattern. They first learn small words, babble and much later understand their meanings. But modern education views this as somewhat regressive—it gives high importance to inquisitive conscious learning. Rote learning is almost a 'no-go' area.

The memory-based learning question can be framed in another way—can the brain learn first mechanically in a subconscious way and our conscious mind (cognitive awareness) assign meaning to it subsequently? To understand it better, it is important to know how human memories work.

Different Types of Memories

We generally think that memory is one homogenous thing. However, there are different types of human memories with their own unique characteristics.

A declarative memory is something that we can articulate and express clearly. I would say it is a kind of conscious memory. We know what we know and can explain the 'why and how' about it. For example, when we read a story book, it gets into our declarative memory and our cognitive faculties are fully aware of the same. In common parlance when we say memory, we generally mean this declarative memory.

The declarative memory is further divided into episodic memory and semantic memory. If someone asks you what you had for dinner yesterday, your brain goes through the episode like where you ate, who all were there and then you recall the dinner as well. This is called episodic memory which is associative. If someone asks you the capital of France, you just say Paris. You don't recall any incident or episode with this. You don't even recall when this information got into your head. This is called semantic memory. Both these form part of the long-term memory. Biologically, long-term memory is dispersed in different parts of the cortex; there is no central location for its storage.

There is another type of memory related to our skills that we learn. We know how it is done but we can't explain. This is called procedural memory —a form of memory that we can't articulate, but our neurons in the brain learn by themselves by watching our body perform those actions. This appears weird as if neurons were some sentient beings, but that's how it works. Any skill for example, playing tennis, swimming, playing guitar or riding a horse is learnt this way. They are difficult to explain in words. Try to teach how to tie the shoelaces to your child only by speaking, without any action—it will be virtually impossible. We will have to act it out because we don't consciously know how we do it.

If you ask a tennis player how he hits the perfect ace at the exact angle and right velocity, he may be completely clueless about it. The neurobiological fact is that the ace player is not aware of how he plays tennis, but the millions of neurons in his brain know exactly how to fire in sequence, and order commands to the hands, legs and body. This part of the memory is stored in the lower back portion of our brain called cerebellum. Essentially, the procedural memory never gets into our cognitive awareness or consciousness. This form of procedural memory is called muscle memory.

We get amazed at the sight of jugglers and wonder how effortlessly he juggles objects. When we try to do the same, we struggle and find it an impossible task. Our conscious mind tries to keep track of the different moving parts, and the more we think, the more difficult it is. But the crux of the problem is in practicing it enough times so that this process becomes subconscious. Our muscles learn of their own, perform in a sequence and we are not aware of it. The same thing happens when we learn driving—our conscious brain is busy coordinating the hands, legs and eyes, only to feel exhausted. Once we learn to drive subconsciously, we are no longer tensed—we listen to music and talk to our fellow passengers as our eyes, hands, legs and ears do their job effortlessly in perfect harmony with each other.

Have you ever walked from one room to another room and then forgot why you went there (and then go back to the earlier room hoping you will remember it again there)? You walk into the kitchen, open the fridge door and suddenly forget what you wanted. You wanted to get something but can't remember, somehow? It happens many times with us that we suddenly lose our train of thought and keep wondering what we were thinking about, a few minutes back. It is a very restless feeling till we recall what we were thinking earlier. Well, none of these are any signs of old age memory loss, this is how our 'working memory' works.

Working memory deals with the task of the moment. It is continually at work. It never shuts down. This is what we call thinking, in a way. It is very agile and flexible. However, it has a severe limitation—it is very short. Many neurological experiments show that the working memory can only hold 4 (some claim 7) items at one time. It appears ridiculous that our working memory could be so limited. You can easily prove that in a day-to-day experiment. Tell anyone a list of 5 unrelated items (e.g., shoes, jungle, highway, table, book), the next moment ask him to do a multiplication (e.g., 23X19) and read out the last 7 alphabets in reverse order. Now ask him to name the 5 items that was told to him. In most experiments, people can remember only 4.

The working memory is like a scratch pad that gets over-written every few moments. It has a very short life. The reason it is still so effective is that it augments itself with the pre-acquired knowledge of long-term memory. It is the orchestrator that taps into all different types of memory, momentarily. For example, when we speak, the working memory connects with the long-term memory of words and semantics on the spur of the moment. It makes it look like a uniform flow.

The working memory is the most important in development of math skills and cognitive abilities i.e., human intelligence. It is the ability to hold the context together and synthesise information quickly before it gets cleaned up. Some educationists recommend active intervention to enhance this ability at an early age. People with more working memory are more likely to be writers, thinkers and probably more intelligent than the rest. Working memory is the closest explanation of what we call 'consciousness'.

How short-term memory is transferred to long-term memory is one of the least-known areas of brain science. The brain does not transfer all short-term memory to long term, only the salient events are transferred. For example, you may not recall what you ate for dinner 25 days back, but if it was your birthday, you will recall that. It seems the brain assigns some salience index to each memory and only the significant ones are transported to long-term memory. One speculation is that this happens when we sleep—the hippocampus in our brain transfers the day's significant events to different cortex areas. This could be the reason that often people with insomnia suffer from poor memories. So, if you want a good memory, you must sleep well.

If memory is so critical for our intelligence, one would like to have as much of it as possible—why not a photographic memory?

Story of Rebecca: When you Have Photographic Memory

We always think that forgetting things is problematic. Of course, it is. But there is a bigger problem if one doesn't forget at all. Imagine someone having imprinted in their memory, every detail of everyday events. The neuroscientists call this HSAM—Highly Superior Autobiographical Memory and, rarely, some people exhibit these symptoms. A person with this photographic memory can walk out of an art exhibition recording every detail, and possibly reproduce them exactly. If nothing else, we would have craved to have this quality during our exam time in school days. The ability to remember everything could have made us god-like, a walking Google.

People suffering from this disorder, however, explain it otherwise. They say that it has made their lives horrible. The problem with such a blessing or disorder is that life can get stuck and repeat itself like a broken record. All memories come with a package of associated emotions. One can't think about past events without feeling good, sad, angry or nostalgic about them.

Rebecca Sharrock, one of the persons diagnosed with the disease says that she not only remembers all the events crystal clear since she was three years old, but she is forced to go through her emotional response as a child even when she has grown up now. It means that if she threw a tantrum if someone denied her a chocolate when she was three, even as an adult she would have an overpowering urge to repeat that response on such a stimulus. This practically forces her to behave like a child even though she has outgrown childhood. Some of these people are likely to develop various neurological illnesses.

Story of HM: when you can't form new memories

Most research on memory in neuroscience have come from experiments on a single person known by his initials HM. He suffered a skull fracture during his childhood which resulted in him having epileptic seizures. This problem became so severe that HM could not continue his studies. He could not even live a normal life. As a last resort, doctors operated on his brain and cut off some parts of it—part of the temporal lobes and two small limbic organs called the hippocampi. The surgery was successful, and HM stopped having seizures.

Thankfully, HM's epilepsy was cured. However, he started suffering from a peculiar problem. He could not form new memories from the date of his surgery. If a doctor met him in the morning and the same doctor met him in the evening, HM could not know if he was the same person. He could watch the same movie many times without realising that he had seen that already. He forgot that he had a meal soon after eating. He could eat multiple times. This led the neuroscientists to believe that the portion of the brain that was operated on, i.e., the hippocampus and temporal lobe are somehow connected with creation of new memories.

Apparently, HM lived a happy life till he died in 2008 at the age of 82 years. A doctor who was working with him explained that except for the short-term memory issue, HM was fine. He was never bored because every experience was a new experience for his brain. Surprisingly, HM remembered most of the things before the surgery. This led the neuroscientists to believe that short-term and long-term memories are stored differently in the brain. While the short-term memory is stored in the hippocampus, the long-term memory is stored in different parts of the cortex in a diffused way. This led to the conclusion that even when some part of the brain is damaged, the overall long-term memory is still preserved through the other part of the cortex, though the quality of memory comes down.

The human stories on memories prove that either extreme of memory power can be problematic. While not being able to remember salient events could be a problem, not able to forget ordinary experiences with a photographic memory could be equally worse. We need a healthy balance of memory and forgetfulness.

The Lost Mariner

Oliver Sacks, in his book *The Man Who Mistook His Wife for a Hat,* talks about the case of one of his patients who was a marine in the Second World War. In 1965 when Oliver met him, the marine displayed peculiar behaviour. He did not recall what happened the last 20 years but had crystal clear memory till 1945. When Oliver showed him a picture of Earth possibly taken from the moon, he refused to believe that humans had already landed on the moon. He recognised his brother but always asked why he looked so old. His last image was frozen when his brother was still 20 years old. He could not form any new memory since then.

Oliver, as a neuropsychologist, explains this as 'retrograde memory' which is different from a typical memory loss. He goes on to explain how meaningless life can get when time is frozen like that. Memory is the narrative that we set for ourselves; it defines our identity. When this narrative is disrupted, our entire existence is a struggle.

Brain Memory as Computer Memory

If we think that our memory is somewhat like computer memory, we can't be farther from the truth. A computer memory is a combination of address value pair which is encoded in the silicon bits. If we need to access that memory, we only need to know the address. On the contrary, human memory is not stored as an address value pair. Human memory is associative, which means that one property leads to another related property. This is the reason when we recall a past memory, it is never in isolation. If we remember an embarrassing moment at some birthday party, we also recall the colour of the cake, the location it happened, the people who laughed and endless details about the event. A computer memory never bothers about all the associative details.

Another difference is in the storage capacity of memory in human versus the computer. The long-term memory in humans has no known limit. People have been able to memorise many books without their memory failing them. This is where human memory beats the computer memory hands down. All that we will have to tell our brain is that the information is significant (by repeating it several times), and our brain creates connections at synapses to encode this information.

The most significant difference, however, is the way our memory is manipulative. Think of a computer memory that first decides the importance of the event, discards the insignificant ones and alters the values in other cases before storing them. In software programming, such a computer memory would be junked, but this is how human memory works. The brain first selects the information that needs to be stored (salience) and discards the insignificant ones. Not only that, while storing. it alters the real event to add an egocentric bias, what is called 'memory bias'. This is the reason when we recall past events, we see ourselves being the most important actor in those events while the truth could have been that we might have been just an insignificant observer.

One of the jobs of our brain is to inflate our ego by exaggerating the significance of our actions. For our brain, we are the heroes. The story is altered if it does not fit the same. But this also means that our memories are fallible, and they can't be relied upon.

False Memory

Can we plant a false memory in someone?

Psychologist Loftus and her student Jacqueline selected a set of 24 subjects aged 18–53 for a unique experiment. They told the subjects that they had discussions with their parents/elders and had prepared a list of childhood events of the individual subjects. The subjects were supposed to identify the event as 'true' or 'false' and describe them in some detail. One of the events mentioned was 'lost in the mall and getting rescued by an elder'— only that it was planted among several other true events. Surprisingly 6 out of 24 recalled that as a true event and went on to describe in detail, something that possibly never happened. They embellished the incidents with absolutely imagined events.

This experiment was repeated with several other false events like taking a hot air balloon ride, being hospitalised overnight, and being a victim of a vicious animal attack. In all the cases, the experimenters were able to create false memories in a significant number of cases. This brings into question how much a person's memory should be relied on, especially for something as crucial as courtroom witnesses.

During the 1980s in the United States, there was a mass hysteria created by the infamous McMartin preschool sexual abuse. The trial did not find anyone guilty, but it created a large number of reported cases of repressed memories. This was followed by some nationwide surveys that said '1 in 3 girls have been molested within the family'. Meredith Maran, a journalist accused her father of abuse at the age of 37 years. 10 years later, she recanted her statement saying it was a false memory. She wrote an infamous book, *My Lie: A True Story of a False Memory*. Some people criticise psychotherapy precisely for this reason— it can plant false memories at the repeated insistence of the psychotherapist.

Another way to manipulate the subconscious memory is to show images to people for a very short time so that it does not get into their awareness but indirectly influences their actions. In the advertising world, it is known as subliminal marketing. This originated in 1957 when a market researcher James Vicary inserted the words, 'Hungry? Eat popcorn and drink Coca-Cola' into a movie for a flash of 0.03

seconds. In that short exposure, it does not register in our conscious memory and we don't know if we have seen these words. However, Vicary claimed that this increased the sale of popcorn by 57.5 per cent and Coca-Cola by 18.1 per cent. Though the results were disputed, this opened the ethical topic of manipulating human minds without them being aware of the same. It is still used by some marketers.

The brain also stores the events that has high emotional content. People remember in amazing detail every detail of an unfortunate car accident, for example. Such events get imprinted like crystal clear images. The brain does this to make sure we remember it well and prevent it from happening again. But this imprint becomes so strong at times that it interferes with the normal functioning of the brain. In some traumatic cases, the repeated flash of the unfortunate event makes it even more difficult to recuperate emotionally.

We all know how difficult life can get when memory fails us. Despite all fallibility, memory is something that defines who we are. Without memories, there will be no identities. This is tragically evident for people suffering from Alzheimer's disease. In such cases, there is an overall degradation in the glial cells in the brain that makes the retrieval of information difficult. People forget their homes, can't identify their loved ones, and slowly lose the emotional connections of the world around them. This is one of the most pressing challenges for medical science today.

Key learnings:

1. Our memory defines our character. It threads different events in a way that gives us a sense of continuity. We feel we are the same person, even though mentally and biologically we change every moment.

2. Sudden loss of long-term memory makes up for a good storyline but is highly unlikely because the long-term memory is not localised in one area in our brain but spread across the entire cortex.

3. Memory is not just the conscious information we remember; it also consists of muscle memory that we can't articulate but our brain knows. Working memory is another type of memory that defines our thinking process and intelligence. Our working memory is very short, but it latches on to our long-term memory to achieve complex cognitive tasks.

4. Though we are often tempted to compare, our memory is not like computer memory. Memory has a strong egocentric bias to store

only important information. It changes the information in a way that we feel we are at the centre of things. The memory makes us the hero even when we might have been just a side actor.

5. Memory is not always reliable. Many psychological experiments have shown that a memory can be planted falsely. We can imagine things that never happened, subconsciously making them a part of our memory.

6. While not being able to form a new memory can be devastating, a photographic memory can be equally problematic. For healthy living, we need to have a proportionate mix of both the skills—the ability to remember and equally important ability to forget.

7. Healthy sleep is the one of the most essential reasons for good memory. This is the time when significant events of the day are transferred to long-term memory and get encoded. People who suffer from insomnia are more likely to have poor memories.

8. Long-term memory for humans has no known limitations. People can store multiple books in their brain. If we practice well, we

can master any skill which eventually gets stored as procedural memory. Memory like most other brain functions work on the principle of 'use it or lose it'.

9. Memory is something that makes us human. Scientifically, we have still very limited knowledge on how our memory is encoded, stored and retrieved in our brain.

10. When the memory functions fail, we lose our sense of identity and emotional connect with the world around us. That is why a disease like Alzheimer's turns out to be so devastating.

Why Do We Feel for Others?

I do not ask the wounded person how he feels, I myself become the wounded person.

—Walt Whitman, 'Song of Myself'

Imagine you are in a jungle resort for a holiday. After a very refreshing experience and day-long trekking, you are back in your room. You are about to go to bed when you notice a breaking news on television that a lion has trespassed into the resort area, causing panic among the residents. You feel fortunate and relieved that you are safe inside your room. However, suddenly you hear a frenzied knock on your door, a person pleading with you to let him come inside your room. You sense the person could be in danger, hence you must open the door. While you do that, mind you, there is also a real possibility that the lion can sneak in and attack you.

What will you do—open the door or not? Will you risk your own life to save an unknown person?

You may do whatever you want but can't deny a strong urge to save the person from danger, even when it means some danger to you. It appears that when any person is in pain, it creates a corresponding pain in us and eventually forces us to act—it is called empathy.

The early philosophers believed that empathy emerged from the kindness of the heart. They thought that our heart is very sensitive to the suffering of others and reciprocates the same emotions. These emotions are what make us humans.

In most of early literature, we always find the heart being given more importance than any other organ in the body when it comes to certain emotions. The early philosophers also believed that all our thoughts emanate from the heart. Aristotle went to the extent of saying that the seat of the human consciousness was our heart and not the brain. According to him, the purpose of the brain was to keep the heart cool just like the radiator of a car. With so many capillary-like structures, it is understandable how early philosophers, even someone like Aristotle might have got deluded to believe the supremacy of heart in cognitive functions. It is not just a coincidence that the symbol of love (the most powerful human emotion) is the heart.

The discovery of brain science later proved that Aristotle was way off the mark on this topic. The real seat of human consciousness is the brain. Our brain creates all thoughts, emotions and cognitive functions. In fact, the heart plays no role in this regard. It is the purpose of our heart to supply clean and cool blood to our brain to function efficiently. Aristotle wrongly got it the other way around. The fact is that our mind is like the engine of the car and the heart is the radiator. The brain is home to all our emotions and intelligence.

The seat of the human soul if at all anything, is the brain. The heart is an important organ like the liver or kidney, but it has no role to play in defining our behaviour. Even after this scientific discovery, our fascination with the heart has not gone away. Even today, some people believe that artists and poets think from their heart while the rest of us think from our brain— the heart is the nice guy and has empathy while the brain is scheming, cunning, and ready to hoodwink others. We often say in a dilemma— 'do what your heart says'.

However, today with some understanding of neurons and the electric activities in them, this debate is settled, that not only empathy but all human emotions emanate from the brain. So, the next time your heart starts pounding when you propose to your girlfriend, blame your brain, not your heart for that. The heart is only reacting to the hormonal flow triggered by your brain.

Coming back to empathy—when we see someone in pain, we feel the pain as if it is hurting us indirectly. The first reaction is to help the person, not only to help him or her get rid of the pain but to also relieve ourselves of the agony. Some emotions in us connect us universally with every other human being, even when they are completely unknown to us. The word 'humanity' reflects this feeling. We see every other human being as some extension of our own self. Though it may not be 100 per cent true in all situations (otherwise there would be no murder or violence by fellow humans), but largely true.

Some of us even extend this to all living beings, including animals and plants. This brings up the concept of collective well-being of all organisms on this planet. The age-old Indian philosophy calls this *Vasudhaiv Kutumbham,* which means that the entire universe is one family. In ancient Vedic literature, social well-being was considered as important as the individual well-being. This is encapsulated well in

sarve bhavantu sukhinaḥ
sarve santu nirāmayāḥ
sarve bhadrāṇi paśyantu mā kaścidduḥ khabhāgbhaveta

(May all sentient beings be at peace, may no one suffer from illness, may all see what is auspicious, may no one suffer)

Why Do We have Empathy?

At the outset, it could be an evolutionary gift. A larger tribe has better chances to protect itself and reproduce. Even animals prefer to be in their herds and protect each other, but humans have been exemplary in this regard. We have the unique ability to transpose ourselves into any other person and feel the same way that he or she might feel. Psychologists also explain this as '*theory of mind*'.

Every normal human mind understands that it has thoughts, beliefs, intents, emotions, knowledge, etc., and at the same time it can also attribute these mental states to others. In simple terms, we believe just as we have a mind, everyone else has one as well. We don't stop here. We bother about what the other mind thinks about us and it affects our own subjective well-being. We tend to act in a way so that other minds think positively of us, which makes us happy. By helping others, we can surely presume that the other persons will reflect positively on us.

Evolutionary theory for development of empathy is fine, but does empathy have any scientific basis?

In 1992, a team of neuroscientists led by Giacomo Rizzolatti inserted tiny electrodes into the brains of macaque monkeys to understand how the brain orchestrates the movement of hands. They indeed found the neurons that fired when the monkeys were doing some physical activity. This was along the expected lines as the premotor cortex fires up before firing the motion command to the hands. This was just one part of the experiment.

One day while the students were having lunch, they sensed that neurons in a monkey's brain fired even though the monkey was motionless. This was serendipity. When the scientists explored further, they discovered that the monkey had certain neurons that fired irrespective of whether the activity was performed by itself or when it saw some other monkey performing that activity—moving of hand during eating in this case.

This led to the discovery of what we call 'mirror neurons'. Mirror neurons are activated both when an individual performs a motor act or observes another performing a motor act. These neurons in our brain also fire when we see someone in pain as it stimulates the similar pain circuit in our brain. It is a sort of virtual reality for our brain. It recalls the similar experience it might have had in the past and replays when it sees someone else in that situation. So, this essentially means that the empathy comes from these neurons.

What happens when these mirror neurons are damaged? Some neuroscientists believe that cases of autism have this underlying malfunction of mirror neurons. Their brains lack the ability to simulate the emotional state of other brains and hence, they don't reciprocate. So, next time your girlfriend blames you for not reciprocating to her feelings, you can turn back and say—'well you know, it's not my fault, it is due to my mirror neurons going crazy'.

If we extend the logic of mirror neurons further (something like excessive empathy), we will encounter another unexpected problem. Imagine you are watching someone eat food and if your neurons can fire as if you are eating, it may dissuade you from getting food for yourself. You may die hungry while your brain may keep sending signals of eating. There is another set of neurons that inhibits those mirror neurons to not get carried away. Too much empathy could be bad for your own survival, as they say in the flight announcement, 'During any emergency first put your own oxygen mask before helping others'.

Though the discovery of mirror neurons is not fully understood or universally accepted by all neurologists, it does provide some scientific basis for our unique ability to feel (hence the word vicarious) the emotion that the other persons might be experiencing. We empathise with them. This may appear a small thing in isolation, but empathy could be the single most reason why we help and cooperate with fellow human beings.

In fact, humans cooperate with each other like no other species do. They have formed communities to help each other. They have realised that there was greater value in cooperation than conflict. This possibly was the underlying basis of establishment of our civilisation and our ability to survive collectively till this age.

This does not mean that humans have been the most peaceful species to co-exist. In fact, human history is full of violence and wars since time immemorial. We have brutally killed each other and made several species extinct. We have been barbaric and merciless at times. Some historians believe that the homo sapiens killed all other form of early humans like the neanderthal. They killed everyone who posed even a small threat to them. They even killed each other to set up empires, win territories or sometimes just to prove their might. This has happened in pre-historic times, during medieval times and is even happening now. No other species have been so violent. Animals kill other animals mainly for food or to protect themselves from being prey, but humans can kill others for a variety of reasons, including for fun.

Do you see this dichotomy? On one hand, we say that humans have cooperated the most, thanks to their empathy, and on the other hand, they have also been the most barbaric.

I think that we have empathy for people who we call our own 'tribe' but little regard for the ones whom we do not identify with. We cooperate more with people who are like us, e.g., friends and families and extend this concept to other entities like race, communities, cities, religion, country, etc. However, we fiercely compete with people who are not like us, e.g., different country, community, religion or race. There is no empathy for humans from the competing group. Darwin's evolutionary theory says that competition and cooperation both are required for the progress of the species. The weaker groups must exit the gene pool for the fittest to survive. Going by this logic, cooperation and competition were the different sides of the same coin furthering a common objective.

Let us see how people behave differently in a group and if there is something called groupthink.

In 1971, Stanford University did a famous (or some call it infamous) prison experiment to check if similar people behave differently when they are part of different groups.

During the summer break, Prof. Philip Zimbardo had set up a small prison at the basement of the university building where makeshift prison cells were set up. The students were invited to be part of a behavioural study. For most of them, a 15 dollar per day payout was not a bad deal as such. The 24 selected students were divided randomly into two groups—12 of them were asked to be prisoners while the remaining 12 were identified as the guards. Both the groups were told that they would be observed through cameras as they were part of the study. The experiment was planned for 2 weeks.

The observers noticed that the guards started becoming harsh with the prisoners. They started controlling every move of the prisoners. The prisoners felt that they were treated badly. They planned a rebellion. The guards on the other hand reciprocated with even harsher measures. The situation escalated to such a damaging level during the experiment that the participants had emotional breakdowns.

When the professor explained this situation to his girlfriend, who herself was a psychologist, she blasted him for such an unethical experiment. Later, many other professors called out this experiment as being unethical and harsh on the subjects. The experiment was called off on the sixth day, much before the planned completion of two weeks. There are documentaries made on this experiment.

There were many conclusions from this experiment that are key findings in psychology textbooks. One of them is that even normal people when part of different competing groups can be extremely harsh with each other. In this experiment, the prisoners and captors were part of random groups with no specific background in crime or patrolling. They all knew that they were part of an experiment and the whole thing was not real. Still the captors behaved in a very harsh manner leading to the prisoners' revolt. Their empathy was completely missing. When the Abu Ghraib scandal broke out in Iraq, the psychology professors explained that as the Stanford experiment playing out in real life. When we are in a group, we behave differently, the groupthink trumps empathy.

Similar observations were recorded from the prisoners in concentration camps during the Second World War. As a practice, the Germans used to select a few among the Jewish prisoners and elevate them as guards. Under normal circumstances, these Jewish guards could be expected to empathise with the prisoners more, and possibly be kind to them. The observed behaviour was entirely opposite. As soon as the prisoner was promoted as a guard, his behaviour changed entirely. In fact, most of them were harsher and crueller than the German guards. This only shows that we are more likely to adhere to our expected group and compete fiercely with the competing group.

An incident in 1960 and associated psychological experiments brought up a new aspect of social behaviour.

> In 1964, Kitty Genovese, a 28-year-old young woman was walking back to her apartment building in New York relatively late in the evening. She parked her car about 100 yards from her apartment and started walking towards the entrance. At this time, Winston Moseley attacked her with knives. She screamed for help. Since it was a warm summer night, apartments had their windows open. As per a *New York Times* report, 38 people heard or saw Kitty being attacked but none of them came forward to help her or called the police. The attacker ran away when Kitty screamed.
>
> As Kitty was walking towards her apartment, she found the apartment building door locked and at this point she collapsed. Unfortunately, the attacker returned after ten minutes and this time he attacked her several times. A witness who heard the scream the second time finally called the police, but it was too late and Kitty was dead.

This single murder became very sensational because it depicted how cold a city could be when your own neighbours refuse to help. Those were the days of rapid urbanisation in the United States, and people took it as the unwanted outcome of leaving the small setup of their villages where everyone helped the other person. 'City life is going to be impersonal and de-humanised'—many newspaper headlines claimed. Many agreed that this is the cost we must pay to live in the large cities. City folk don't care. It was the sad reality of urbanisation.

Some of the psychologists were not convinced with this simplistic conclusion. John Darley and Bibb Latane from Columbia University set up an experiment where they invited students for an interview. While the students waited for their turn in the waiting room, a controlled smoke emission was set up from under the door to signify the fire breakout. The psychologists wanted to check how the students reported the event. The experiment was done in two different setups—when the student was alone and when they were in a group.

The findings were startling. When the student was alone, he almost invariably reported the incident of fire. When they were in a group, the students saw the smoke, looked at each other but in nine out of ten cases they did not report the incident.

The above experiment was conducted in many different forms and each time the conclusion was the same—people in a group suffer from what is known in psychology as the 'bystander effect'. This is explained as 'diffusion of responsibility' in a large group. The psychologist explained that Kitty could have been saved if fewer people had seen her being attacked. This appears counter-intuitive, but we have a larger sense of responsibility when we see things as individuals or in very small groups. In a larger group, we don't act proactively, thinking we may not be the best person to intervene and someone else should.

Haven't we read how sometimes a mob gathers around an injured person in a road accident and instead of promptly helping the person, they just watch. Or worse, they capture selfies with the injured. We observe what the other people are doing in the situation and just follow them. If no one is helping, we also adopt the same approach. These are the situations when the groupthink overrides the individual emotions of sympathy.

To understand how people behave in a group, in 1954, a team of psychologists brought together a team of pre-teen schoolboys to a summer camp at Robber's Cave State Park in Oklahoma. They created two groups randomly and gave them fancy names. One group was called Eagles while the other was called Rattlers. They were not given any specific information on how to deal with each other.

The researchers observed that soon a strong prejudice was formed between the groups. It started with light name-calling and taunting but very soon it got more serious. The Eagles torched the Rattlers' flag and next day the Rattlers plundered the Eagles' cabin, flipped over their beds and stole their clothing. Soon, the groups became so hostile to each other that the researchers had to physically segregate them. When the students were asked to describe the attributes of the groups, they offered quite flattering terms for their own group and heaped insults on the other.

The conclusion from the experiment made the researchers believe that antagonism can emerge from arbitrary divisions.

In the second part of the experiment, the psychologists tried to unite these two groups by removing their prejudices. They gave both the groups a common enemy. The biases subsided though they did not vanish completely.

Our urge to comply with the group is so strong that we override our own conclusions. There was a famous lab experiment done by Solomon Asch in 1950 among the students of Swarthmore College in the United States.

As part of a vision test, a group of 50 male students were shown 3 lines drawn on a paper and asked to identify the smallest of the 3. All the group members except 1 (who was the real subject of the experiment, others were just co-conspirators assisting the study) were asked to wrongly identify the smallest line. The objective was to understand if the subject would go by his own judgement of the smallest line or go by the group judgement (even when it was evidently wrong).

When the real subject was asked to identify the smallest line, in 75 per cent of the cases, he just went by the group and defied his own observation. When the subject was interviewed later as to why he wrongly identified, he responded that he really did not believe his conforming answer but had to go along with the group for the fear of being ridiculed or being peculiar. This experiment demonstrates that we are more than willing to doubt our own judgement to comply with the groupthink.

If you are still not convinced of how the groupthink can cloud our own judgement, you can do a small experiment with your peer group (within close friends). First, pick one unsuspecting member as the subject of the exercise. A new member in the group is the best bet as he tries the most to conform to the group. Tell all other group members (except the subject) beforehand that you are going to tell a very flat joke (no joke actually—but a bland sequence of random statements) but all of them are supposed to burst into laughter. They have to say this is the best joke they have ever heard. The joke needs to be told in front of the unsuspecting member of the group.

The new person (subject) clearly knows that it is not a joke at all, but he gets terribly confused by everyone else bursting into laughter. After a few seconds, he starts laughing as well. He agrees with his friends that this is the best joke he has ever heard. It works almost every time, provided the subject is not aware of this plot. It is great fun to watch the person override his own sense of humour judgement and believe that the joke is funny and somehow try to laugh. This is called peer pressure, opposite of the bystander effect.

The 'in-group' and 'out-group' phenomenon explains why we feel so much empathy for people of our group. But is there a neurological basis for that?

There was an experiment conducted on a group of 105 individuals while they were under fMRI scanner. The researchers deceptively told them that they were recruited for studying the relationship between memory and pain. The real objective was to understand the neural empathic response. Each of them was shown pictures of human hands on a computer screen, one by one. Every time, the hand was marked with a label—Christians, Hindus, Muslims, Jews, Atheists and Scientologists. When the subject saw a hand, they also knew (going by the label) if it was a Christian hand, Muslim hand, Hindu hand and so on. As a part of the experiment, they pricked the hand in the picture and measured the neural response from the scanner.

The experimenters concluded that when the subject was a Christian and the hand shown was marked as Christian, a prick on this hand activated the same region of the brain as if the person himself was getting pricked. In the case of the hands of another group, this region was not equally activated. This same observation was repeated for subjects of other religions as well.

This experiment led to the conclusion that 'in-group' and 'out-group' construct has a neurological basis. This was an important finding on how our brain re-organises itself to empathise with those we relate to. This can also explain why there is so much of polarisation in social and political lives these days. If we look at the social media, on every issue there are extreme opinions that never converge.

The space for rational conversation is shrinking increasingly and we may have little control over it.

Key takeaways in our daily lives:

1. Human empathy is the unique gift of our brain using which we can vicariously experience the emotions of other minds. Psychologists call this 'theory of mind'.

2. Thanks to empathy, humans cooperate with each other which has been the basis of communities and civilisation. This has ensured our survival and reproduction over the years.

3. This empathy is sometimes extended to animals as well. Some religions teach us to have empathy for all living beings.

4. Experiments have shown that empathy is governed by what we call mirror neurons in our brain. These neurons mimic the similar experience as if we are doing the act ourselves.

5. In case of autistic children, these mirror neurons are found to be not functioning properly which is why they are not able to reciprocate their emotions fluently.

6. We have a strong tendency to relate to people who are like us and compete with people who belong to different groups. The Stanford Prison experiment proved that the same set of people can behave in completely opposite manner if part of different groups.

7. While humans have cooperated within their tribes, they have also been one of the most violent species on Earth. It is believed that the homo sapiens killed all other early humans like the neanderthal.

8. A study with the preschool teens showed that students have flattering opinions for the members of the 'in-group' while they were very antagonistic towards the other. This happened even when the group formation was entirely arbitrary.

9. Groupthink and peer pressure trump our individual thinking resulting in what we call 'bystander effect' or 'peer pressure' where we decide our actions based on what others are doing rather than trusting ourselves.

10. The 'in-group' and 'out-group' formation can also explain the extreme polarisation that we have in the social media these days. Neurological experiments have shown that such biases also change the neural structure of our brain.

Fear of a Black Cat

If a black cat crosses your path, it signifies that the animal is going somewhere.

—American comedian Groucho Marx

Have you ever noticed someone walking alone on a road and then he suddenly stops because he sees a black cat crossing the road ahead of him?

The mischievous cat probably knows about this, and I am sure it enjoys the special privilege of right to passage. The person might have broken traffic rules earlier and ignored the traffic police several times, but he can't ignore this tiny cat somehow. He looks around and draws an imaginary line on the road and stops before crossing that line. He patiently waits for someone else to cross that imaginary line before he does. Thank God he was saved of impending bad luck; the person feels relieved. You may call the person superstitious and laugh at him.

Most of the superstitions are so deep-rooted that they have become part of our customs. Sometimes, these superstitions are indistinguishable from our cultural practices. For example, it is difficult to say whether the breaking of a coconut before the start of an auspicious activity for Hindus is a custom or a superstition or both. Some of them also take the form of rituals. Have we not seen people in India using lemons and chillies tied in a string to cast bad luck away? They possibly can't explain how they work and may feel even embarrassed for this behaviour. But they believe that it works, and beliefs force them to act in that way. These beliefs get passed on to multiple generations without much rationalisation.

It is possible that many societies encouraged superstitions to provide a simple handbook to the masses with very simplistic explanations on dos and don'ts. For example, a bat's presence in the house is considered to bring death. Now we know well that bats contain many deadly viruses that have caused many pandemics. Hence, it must have been a healthy practice to stay away from bats. Similarly, ghosts living on *peepal* trees might have been popularised to prevent people sleeping under it at night because it emits carbon dioxide and may cause suffocation to people. It is easier to frighten people with ghost stories rather than explaining scientific concepts to them. For people who don't understand viruses or photosynthesis, the above superstitions may be helpful. However, for most superstitions, there are no scientific explanations. This phenomenon is not limited only to specific cultures, religions or countries. The nature and extent of beliefs differs, but invariably most of us have some beliefs that we know defy any rational logic but we still hold onto them. We inherit some of them but we create many ourselves as well. Do you have a specific pen that helps you answer all the questions in the exam and fetch good marks— that lucky pen? Do you notice that whenever you wore that black colour socks, you were able to score the maximum goals in football? Or that your blue T-shirt helps you win in the casino?

We call them 'lucky shoe', 'lucky shirt', 'lucky bat', 'lucky pen'—the list could be endless. Likewise, there is also a series of unlucky things. This is not only limited to inanimate things. We form similar superstitions about people around us too. Some people we believe are lucky, some are unlucky.

There is a whole field of black magic that is still practiced in many countries even though it is outlawed. Some superstitious people even go to the extreme level, endangering their own lives and that of the people around them. Then there are people who believe that the position of the stars affects their lives.

There is a complete field of formal study around it called horoscopy. It seems, the sun sign and moon sign at the time of birth can predict the nature of the person, including key life events. It is considered so important that it has been used for matchmaking during marriages in India. I will be offending many people if I call them superstitions, but astrology does lack scientific basis so far.

Then there are a bunch of studies on fortune telling—from palmistry to tarot card reading, crystal gazing and card selections by parrots. Many of us might have been keen about palmistry at some point in time—there are a lot of interesting stories that make us believe them. They appear as structured as some of our modern science books. They don't provide practical experimental proofs as in science, but that does not stop palmistry from having millions of followers.

Many religions have rituals that can border on superstitions. So, we might be tempted to conclude that religious people are more likely to be superstitious. However, many atheists who don't believe in God, also seem to have their own superstitions. They may not have religious superstitions but still may have personal superstitions. A gambler who is an atheist may have a strong belief that he wins money at certain slot machines only. Most gamblers have some or the other superstitions. Religious people are more likely to be superstitious, but the other way around may not be true.

When you are waiting for an elevator—have you pressed the elevator button multiple times? It happens with me—first I press the button, then after some time, I press it again and then do it again till finally it arrives. Now here is the point—we all know that the elevators work as per an algorithm and once we press the button, our request is queued in a sequence. Any number of repeat presses does not make it any faster, but we still do that impatiently whether we are in a hurry or not.

The psychologists explain this behaviour differently. When we press the lift button multiple times and when the lift finally arrives, we somehow believe that it was the last button press that brought the lift, not the first one. Some of us believe that the multiple button press does work. This observation is subconsciously stored in our mind and we repeat this behaviour. I am sure the elevator manufacturers keep this in mind while designing the algorithm for the same.

Our superstitious behaviour does not co-relate with the level of education. It can be presumed that as we learn more of experimental science, we discard unfounded beliefs. By that logic, more educated people and accomplished scientists should have less superstitions. The facts tell us otherwise. Even rocket scientists eagerly pray in the temple before the launch of their most important mission. Jack Parsons, a founding member of NASA's Jet Propulsion Lab was reportedly heavily involved in occult practices.

> In Robert Froemke's laboratory at the New York University School of Medicine, there were a group of students and post docs that could be clearly divided into two groups—one who obsessively believed that if they left the experiment hall, it would fail while the other believed that the unmonitored experiment would have higher chances of success as it would not be jinxed.

This is not difficult to believe at all. We sometimes experience that during a gripping cricket match on the last ball. Some of us believe that watching that would win our match, while some believe that not watching them would bring good luck to our favourite team.

It is not only individuals, but organisations and institutions also have superstitions. Some of the most modern high-rise buildings in the world built by tech-savvy architects, do not have a 13th floor. Most hotels rename it to mezzanine because people don't prefer to stay there. Some airlines like Air France and

Lufthansa do not have a 13th row, due to the stigma attached to the number.

All the above facts point in one direction. Is there something intrinsic in our brain that makes us superstitious?

Famous psychologist B F Skinner conducted several experiments among animals to explain how behaviour is formed. He is known to have postulated theories on the conditioning of behaviour based on observations on animals like rats and pigeons. He devised a small box for that, now commonly known as Skinner box. He put the rats inside the box and conditioned their behaviour. He conducted experiments that proved their behaviour can be modified by classical conditioning—for example, a rat after repeated exposure to hearing whistles followed by food will create association of whistles with food.

If the experimental setup is such that when one lever is pressed, a rat can get food and another one can generate an electric shock, the rat learns it soon enough and adapts its behaviour accordingly. It will press the food lever when it is hungry and never presses the lever that generates an electric shock. Skinner proved that a rat can quickly learn the rule of the game by random experimentation. He argued this is how all creatures learn and it was at the heart of the behaviourist theory. All creatures find out the causal relationship between the two events and store it in their brain as part of their learning process.

Though this conditioning theory was well established, Skinner did a somewhat unique experiment with pigeons.

Skinner put few pigeons in a Skinner box and through a separate channel, dropped some food pallet at some fixed intervals, like one minute. Unlike the previous experiments on rats, this did not depend on the behaviour of the pigeons. Irrespective of what the pigeons did, the food pallets were going to be served after a fixed time. Skinner was curious to know how the pigeons react in such situations.

After some time, Skinner saw that the pigeons developed a strange behaviour. One of them, for example, started going around in a circle, which it was not doing before. Another one waited in one specific corner of the box. Skinner noticed that though the food pallet was not dependent on the pigeons' actions, the pigeons developed some weird habits.

Skinner explained this as a theory of superstition—though the act of getting the food pallet was random, pigeons developed a wrong association with the act they were doing just before they got the food pallet. So, if a pigeon was going in circles when the food pallet dropped, it developed an association between the two. It believed that going in a circle caused the food pallet to appear. It kept repeating the behaviour and after a few times, it got reinforced as well, though the act was completely random.

Skinner explained this is how superstitions are formed in humans as well.

Have you looked at the cloudy sky during the day? Do you see faces or a garden or a jungle within a few seconds without any effort? Some people apparently see the face of Jesus on grilled cheese sandwiches or Virgin Mary on a stained wall in the subway. Some believe there must be something very special about the date 11/11/11. Once a fellow passenger on a flight explained to me in detail how her grandmother's mood was closely linked with the phases of the moon.

Why Does the Brain Seek Patterns?

The pattern recognition has been essential for our survival whether it was for identifying food or protecting ourselves from dangerous animals. All living organisms are adept in finding patterns. A countereffect of the same is that our brain does not handle randomness well. Hence, it tries to draw a pattern even among unrelated events. It tries to force a correlation even when there is possibly none. Our brain is obsessively focused on creating a rule even when it may not exist. It tries to connect the brown spots behind the bushes and conclude that it must be a snake.

Suppose the brain surmises that a cyclist that hit you while you were walking on the road was just a random event. If it was a random chance event, then nothing can be done about it. It gives a sense of helplessness to the brain. How do we live in a world that is full of random events (which might be true as well)? Should we just wait for things to happen? Are we the actors of our lives or just acted upon by randomness? Our brain whose prime function is to give us a sense of security and survival finds this very discomforting. We want to be in control of our own lives and surroundings. We feel safe and happy if we believe that we are in perfect control. Our brain is like a lackey that flatters our ego to believe that we are at the centre of the world with immense power to control things. Even if we don't control things, we know how the rules of the game work, our brain assures us.

Hence, to find a reason and pattern behind each event is important for the brain. It gives us false comfort that we can control these events in the future, even though there may not be any correlation between the two. While doing so, the brain can go to the ludicrous extreme of irrationality— like some bad event happened because you wore that unlucky red T-shirt, as that had happened one month back as well. It tries to find all possible correlations—some rational and some completely irrational like the colour of the shirt.

In neuroscience, there is a name for it—'apophenia'. It is the obsessiveness of the human brain to find a pattern or causality where none exists. This is not a pathological condition and is found in common people in varying degrees. However, it can become a problem when such pattern identifications run wild as in the case of schizophrenia.

The concept of *karma* may be just an extension of this concept. When we see a person suffering from a disease or some unfortunate accident, we feel that if it was just a random event, it could happen to anyone of us. This scares us. How do we physically and mentally (in the form of worries) protect ourselves in future? How do we look forward to our lives if it is full of randomness and unpredictability? Why is someone rich and someone poor? Why are some people healthy and some suffering from terminal diseases? The real world is full of extremities, but our brain must find a way to navigate through it.

When we fail to find any direct reason for someone's misery (it could be a random event like being born into a poor family) we conclude it must be his or her *karma*. Some of us even extend this to the extent of the person's previous births. He or she must have done something wrong in the current or past lives. It is just coming back to hit him or her. And then we console ourselves that since we have not done anything wrong in the past, we will be spared of that misery. This reassures us that it would not happen to us. This might look irrational but could well be a coping mechanism of our brain in this uncertain world.

Is the world deterministic or random? This is a deep philosophical debate that has intensely engaged the best scientists of all ages. In the Newtonian world, everything was rule based—laws of motion, gravity, etc. Everything could be exactly measured. If hypothetically, one knew all the particles in the universe and their motion, one could predict all the future events. This was the notion of the deterministic world. Our brain is very relieved with living in such a predictable world. When Niels Bohr and Werner Heisenberg proposed a new quantum theory saying no one can ever measure the exact position and momentum of any particle and laid the basis of the uncertainty principle, Einstein (who was initially a proponent and later a fierce critic of the quantum theory) said, "God does not play dice with the universe." In a most watched heated debate at the historic fifth Solvay conference in 1927 in Brussels, Bohr reportedly told Einstein, "Stop telling God what to do." As per historians, Bohr is believed to have won the debate as the quantum theory is closer to the mathematical outcome, but Einstein's objections continue till today at the philosophical level. Einstein is supposed to have said that 'the more successful the quantum theory becomes, the sillier it looks'. Our brain can't comprehend and accept a quantum world where nothing is exact, and everything is probabilistic. In his book *Fooled by Randomness*, Nassim Taleb argues, "It is only because we fail to understand probability that we continue to believe events are non-random, finding reasons where none exist."

How do storytellers and the news reporters exploit this weirdness of our brain? Two random murders in a week in different parts of the city are unmemorable incidents for our brain. What if the news report mentions that both victims have been killed by a specific pattern of knife attacks? The incidents also happened exactly at the same time of the night and a red handkerchief was found nearby. Now our brain becomes very attentive to the story. Is the same person behind the murders? Is he a psychopath? Is there a political angle to it? There could be innumerable questions hinting at some patterns. The news item becomes very interesting for the brain because it has apparently found a pattern behind it.

This is how the storytellers keep our interest alive in a story. They try to connect different events with a lot of innuendoes. Our brain finds it very exciting. We follow the story till the end to find out what the real reason was. That is why soap operas end the show at the peak inquisitive point so that we tune in to it the next day to find out the 'why'.

This should not be mixed up with the genuine inquiry of things and phenomena. This has been the basis of all scientific advances till date. Humans have an innate urge to experiment and find out the rules of nature. The superstitious brain, however, does not engage in genuine enquiry. Deep within, the cognitive brain knows very well that the superstitious causality enforced by it is wrong. For that reason, sometimes we are even hesitant to express our superstitions to the outside world, lest people think how stupid we are. If anything, superstitions prevent us from doing a genuine enquiry because we try to find a shortcut answer even to profound questions.

We always try to find a reason behind everything. It worries us when we don't find any. Now you can understand why we are so obsessed in finding the meaning of our lives. Could it be just a case of 'apophenia'—trying to assign reason to a random event? Researchers and scientists have long argued that life on Earth is one of the random events that could happen on any other terrestrial body as well, among billions in the universe. However, most of us believe that there is some design in the same and that is why we look for meaning in everything we experience.

Key takeaways for our day-to-day life:

1. Superstition is a wrong association of causality that has no scientific basis at all. Sometimes, we know that one event does not cause the other, still we fall for the same.

2. Superstitions are found in all cultures and countries. Sometimes, they form an inseparable part of our culture and traditions as well. These superstitions are passed on across generations verbally, without any form of documentation.

3. Superstitions are found among people of different backgrounds, be it scientist, artists, poets, religious gurus, poor or rich. Even

atheists and hardcore rationalists have their own superstitions.

4. While some superstitions can be harmless, e.g., a lucky pen, in extreme cases they can lead to dangerous practices like black magic.

5. An experiment conducted by psychologists on pigeons proved that they could learn wrong association and exhibit weird characteristics. The human brain works in a similar way.

6. We live in an uncertain world that has lot of randomness built into it. This brings some uncertainties in our daily lives.

7. Our brain hates uncertainties because it introduces unpredictability and helplessness in dealing with future events.

8. Our brain is obsessively engaged in finding a pattern where none may exist, and it may be a pure random event. In neuroscience, there is a clinical term for this extreme condition called 'apophenia'.

9. The brain's eagerness to find a pattern may have some evolutionary basis as well. When we believe we know the reason (even if falsely) for certain events, we think we are in

control of things. This can give us a sense of safety and security, making us happy.

10. Our excessive focus on finding a reason behind even random events is not necessarily undesirable. The basis of science is genuine enquiry. The superstition is a shortcut method of the brain to delude the real causality.

Why We Procrastinate?

People are frugal in guarding their personal property; but as soon as it comes to squandering time, they are most wasteful of the one thing in which it is right to be stingy.

—Seneca

Do you remember a tough course during the college days? The syllabus is already provided one year in advance. The professors take classes regularly during the entire duration of the course. They also advise us to prepare for the final exam by studying periodically. They warn us not to take the course lightly as many students fail.

Then we tell our friends—"Which fool studies so early for exams? There are so many other interesting things to do." Our playful mind is successful in convincing us that we will handle the exams later. We will cross the bridge when we come to it. The professor's warning has no effect.

The weeks and months pass by. One day, suddenly we notice that the exam dates are announced, and they are just a few days away. We have not even started studying. We are not even sure if we have all the class notes. We beg other friends to share their notes.

We recall the professor's warning how many students had failed in the subject last year. Something strange happens to us. The panic dragon in our mind suddenly wakes up. It drives the playful monkey in us away, the one who was responsible for the procrastination. The panic dragon then works out a very stringent plan for the remaining days before the exams— no movies, no games, no TV—only study all day. The panic dragon also keeps us awake the whole night. The most basic need of the human body—food, is also deprioritised.

The interesting thing is, this does not happen just once, but year after year. It seems we never learn (well, most of us; we know some people defy this rule, those topper types).

The panic dragon is very cruel. Still, we must thank it. It is due to this panic dragon that most of us pass the exam and get graduation certificates. The point to note is that it takes control only in case of things like critical exams. If the goal is trivial, e.g., wake up at 5 a.m. every day and go for jogging or join a gym—the playful monkey in us keeps postponing the target forever. The panic dragon never wakes up (unless there is some health emergency and doctors prescribe the mandatory exercise) in such cases.

When it comes to procrastination, there are two types of activities where our mind behaves differently. One, where the goal is externally enforced and the other where the goal is self-managed. A true rational mind does not relinquish its control in either case, be it for the playful monkey or the panic dragon. In the long term, both are bad—while the first one wastes time, the second one wastes our cognitive resources to make us exhausted and anxious. A trained mind works like a seasoned captain that keeps the ship steady, most importantly in the right direction.

What is Procrastination?

It is very easy to define 'procrastination' because it is the disease that we all suffer from, in various degrees. We have been a procrastinator at some point in time or the other. The word is derived from the Latin word *procrastinatum*—'deferred till the morning'. It is the act of intentional delay in starting or finishing a task, knowing well that it will have negative consequences for us. While procrastinating, we overrule our rational judgement which is problematic. In the Bhagavad Gita, Sri Krishna uses the word

Dirghsutri for such people. One of the advices from the sages in ancient India has been *Dirghsutri vinashayati* (A procrastinator does harm to himself).

'I will do it later'—this is the most common thought that most of us grapple with. That 'later' can be captured in the following time series equation:

$$t = t + 1$$

Here the variable 't' keeps changing and the hours turn into days, weeks, months and years. The above mathematical expression stays intact, as in the start. Our mind has a very convenient way to postpone things for the future that never comes. Deep within, we all know that this practice is unhelpful, but we invariably succumb to it.

The good thing about the human mind is that it is pretty much goal-centric. A rational brain dislikes the randomness, so it tries to control things. It plans and executes things systematically to bring in the much-needed predictability. This is the reason human minds have achieved great success. Though we can very effectively set targets for others, our brain faces a unique challenge when it tries to set rules for itself.

Procrastination as an evil has been captured well in the below Sanskrit shloka.

ālasyam hi manuṣhyāṇām sharīrastho mahānripu |
nāstyudyamasamo bandhuḥ kritvā yam nāvasīdati

(Laziness or procrastination is the greatest enemy residing in our own body. There is no good friend like hard work, doing which no one declines.)

There is also a practical version of the same as explained by Kabir: -

kaal kare so aaj kar, aaj kare so ub,
pal mein pralaya hoyegi, bahuri karoge kub

(Tomorrow's work do today, today's work do now. You can never predict what disaster may happen next moment, when will you do the work then?)

The above saying was so apt that it was repeated by the teachers and elders, umpteen number of times, whenever someone tried to postpone anything. Thanks to the repeated quotations, the lazy folks came out with a counter version of the verse as a mark of protest:

aaj kare so kal kar, kal kare so parson
itni jaldi vyarth hai, jab jeena hai abhi barson

(Today's work we should do tomorrow, tomorrow's work, day after. Why should we hurry for everything when we have to live for years?)

The above verse is frivolous, and someone might have created it just for fun to capture the predicament of the lazy people. However, it is equally popular as Kabir's verse, meaning that most people identify themselves with the habit of postponing things than doing them in the timely manner.

'Plenty of Time' Conundrum

Professor of psychology at Duke University, Dan Arierly conducted an experiment with his students.

> He gave his students three assignments and let them set their own deadline of when they wanted to submit them. As students, we can all guess when most of them would have wanted to submit it—well, the last day of the term. But his experiment concluded that the students who provided an earlier deadline did a far better job at the assignment. By planning things earlier, we do a better job.

We are unlikely to start an activity if we believe we have far too much time on hand. There is a common saying that people who stay closest to the airport are more likely to miss their flights than those who stay farther away. This is called 'plenty of time' procrastination.

As an apologist of procrastination, we may well argue that it is a harmless habit, even helpful at times to reduce our anxiety levels. It does not matter when the activity gets done, as long as it gets done. In the corporate world, there is a common saying that 'work expands with time'. If one starts early on, it takes a longer time to complete the task, while those who do that in the last moment, are more efficient. 'People work better under pressure and stiff deadlines,' many bosses believe.

We now have enough evidence to conclude that habitual procrastination can lead to low self-esteem and even depression. Tim Urban, a famous blogger and a TED speaker on the topic, 'Inside a procrastinator's brain' says that we have three conflicting entities in our head.

1. **Instant Gratification Monkey**—We all know them well. They are fun-loving happy creatures who argue against any serious work that may put us under any stress. They always look for an easy way out. This is the monkey that prompts us to watch a YouTube video in the middle of a textbook study. It works on the instant dopamine hit and does not like to wait for anything. It lives in the 'now and here'.

2. **Panic Monster**—This is a no-nonsense taskmaster that does not care about fun or relaxation. It wakes up when the deadline is looming and pumps a good amount of fear in us to make the situation look life-threatening. It does not worry about our comfort and bulldozes us into action without any concern

for consequences. Its only goal is to meet the deadline by hook or by crook. It hates the playful monkey and drives it away like a cruel taskmaster.

3. **Rational Decision Maker**—This is the part of the brain that knows about the above two entities and knows how to keep both at bay. This entity plans for things in advance so that everything gets done in a timely and efficient manner. This requires strengthening our executive brain that activates the rational thinking. The best results in an exam are reserved for these types of students.

Why Does our Mind Love to Procrastinate?

Our mind hates ambiguity. Any new start of an activity brings with itself a lot of uncertainties. The mind loves to deal with the unambiguous things at hand and pushes the new things to the end of the task pipeline. Second, the new things require focused attention which means the mind must deprive itself of the available distractions at hand.

The basic nature of the mind is to be distracted and anything that impedes the distraction is discouraged by it. Our mind in its pure natural form is more like a boat in the deep sea that goes along the force and direction of the waves. Working on a new activity is nullifying the impact of the waves and driving the boat in a specific direction at a steady speed.

The third reason behind procrastination could be anxiety. If the new task is challenging and is going to cause us any anxiety, procrastination is a convenient tool to deal with it. There is a favourite quote that goes well in such situations— 'we will cross the bridge when we come to it'.

We all know we have limited time in life, but we let it tick away. Seneca, a Greek stoic philosopher writes in his 2000-year-old treatise, *On the Shortness of Life:*

> "It is not that we have a short time to live, but that we waste a lot of it. Life is long enough, and a sufficiently generous amount has been given to us for the highest achievements if it were all well invested... So it is: we are not given a short life, but we make it short, and we are not ill-supplied but wasteful of it... Life is long if you know how to use it."

He offers a caution to people who procrastinate by wasting their time.

> "You are living as if destined to live forever; your own frailty never occurs to you; you don't notice how much time has already passed but squander it as though you had a

full and overflowing supply— though all the while, that very day which you are devoting to somebody or something may be your last. You act like mortals in all that you fear, and like immortals in all that you desire... How late it is to begin really to live just when life must end! How stupid to forget our mortality and put off sensible plans to our fiftieth and sixtieth years, aiming to begin life from a point at which few have arrived!"

How Can We Overcome Procrastination?

A very simple answer is just start. Most of the time we keep waiting for a perfect start which is just an excuse to postpone things. There is nothing like a perfect start.

There was an experiment conducted on a set of students who were given certain tasks but were interrupted before they could complete them. They were diverted to another task before resuming the aborted activity. The study revealed that the brain has a greater tendency to finish the task that was started earlier compared to a task that was never started.

The brain tracks the unfinished tasks subconsciously till it completes them. So, if you have been waiting to run a marathon for a long time—a simple advice could be to start with the first 100 metres. Even a tiny start is better than no start.

As the famous quote says, 'journey of the thousand miles start with the first step'. Even if the first step is not in the right direction, with time it can be corrected. Unfortunately, in most cases we keep waiting for the first step forever.

Just like an engine must exert a lot more power when the car needs to be started, a human mind requires a disproportionate amount of will power to get into a new activity. The executive brain in the prefrontal cortex takes up the control in this case. It issues instructions to other parts of the brain to achieve the new goal. This is a conscious process. Slowly, this gets permeated to the other parts of the brain and eventually diffused into the subconscious state. That is when the brain forms it as a habit and the new activity becomes effortless. The brain enjoys the certainty encoded as the habits that becomes the new normal.

For example, if you want to write a book, you can apply this theory. Never wait for the blockbuster idea to come to your mind, it will never come. All you need to do is to focus and write the first page, knowing very well that this could be scrapped later. It is easier to edit a crappy page than to edit a blank page. The first page is important, not its content. The next challenge is to set a ritual to stick to the practice. It could be a certain time in the day when you force yourself to write, come what may. This is the time when your 'monkey mind' tries to distract you the most. But if you continue the ritual for 3–4 weeks, the 'monkey mind' gives up and the practice gets adopted by other parts of the brain. It becomes our habit. That is how mastery over self is achieved and the mind is trained to achieve the desired objectives.

Another approach is to provide positive feedback to our brain even for small achievements. Instead of getting worried about the things we could not achieve, we can focus our attention on the things that we could do. If there were ten activities to be done in the morning today and we could only do two by the end of the day, we can still congratulate ourselves for the two things that we have accomplished. Next day, two can become three and the process can improve till the mind gets used to proper planning and executing to achieve the desired result.

A third approach to beat procrastination is to announce your intentions to other people in advance. This way, the internal goals become external goals. For example, post on Facebook that you are planning to run a 10K marathon next month (presuming you intend to do the same). This sounds exhibitionist but it works. Social pressure works in a positive way in this case. It is like a note to the self but put on the public notice board. You may announce your intent of learning a new subject or topic to your colleagues much in advance. In most cases, your colleagues wouldn't remember but you will have this innate urge to honour the imaginary commitment, and you may be able to beat procrastination this way.

Key takeaways:

1. We all find ourselves guilty of procrastination—delaying a task, knowing well that it may not be the right thing to do. We think it is harmless, but repeated procrastination can affect our well-being and self-confidence.

2. Our brain likes distractions. The instant gratification monkey in all of us keeps pushing the deadline till the panic dragon takes over and sets us on an arduous schedule.

3. A rational brain is the one that understands the nature of the instant gratification monkey and panic dragon. It keeps both away from its sight by proper planning and execution.

4. We are very good at setting goals for others. We are also good at achieving a goal given to us by someone else. However, when we try to set goals for ourselves, in many cases we fare poorly.

5. We procrastinate for various reasons—sometimes just to have some space for fun.

We think we have plenty of time and we will cross the bridge when that comes. Some of us erroneously believe that we are more efficient under pressure.

6. Procrastination can also be a coping mechanism—to avoid anxiety associated with the uncertainty of starting a new task.

7. At times we are so obsessed with finding the perfect time that we forget that an imperfect start is better than a perfect no start.

8. Tip 1 to beat procrastination: **Just start.**

   Our brain keeps tracks of the partly-completed activities till it gets completed. One way to beat procrastination is precisely that—just start the activities without being obsessed with the right timing.

9. Tip 2 to beat procrastination: **Reinforce the small achievements.**

   We need to celebrate activities that we could complete rather than being obsessed with the ones that we have postponed. This is an easy way to build willpower for a rational mind and beat procrastination.

10. Tip 3 to beat procrastination: **Create social promise.**

Announcing of an activity to friends and well-wishers can positively act as a motivator to start the activity. Even social media could be a positive force when we announce our intentions publicly. We are more conscious of the commitment that we make to others than what we make to ourselves.

The War Within our Brain

We're built of contradictions, all of us. It's those opposing forces that give us strength, like an arch, each block pressing the next. Give me a man whose parts are all aligned in agreement and I'll show you madness. We walk a narrow path, insanity to each side. A man without contradictions to balance him will soon veer off.

—Mark Lawrence

Let us imagine a house that was constructed several thousand years back. The architects constructed the house using the best stones available at that time. Since they did not have any sophisticated construction material, the edges were rough and unpolished, but the house was very stable. We started living in the house, one generation after another. Luckily, the house had survived all the earthquakes. It had protected us from heat and rain. It had withstood the natural calamities. The house had also protected us from wild animals. It had done a fantastic job of keeping us safe and secure.

Now imagine that a few hundred years ago, we constructed another floor on this house. By now, bricks and cements were invented so it was used in the construction. It had nicely decorated doors and walls. The flooring was done with marble. This house had basic lighting facilities as well. It had water connections and sanitation facilities. The house had security features. Overall, this floor was much more sophisticated than the ground floor that looked very primitive. We started spending more time on this floor than the cave-like structure on the ground floor.

Next imagine that just a few decades ago, one more floor has been constructed on top of the above house. This floor is like today's smart home. This floor has all modern features like smart lighting and computer- controlled facilities. It has electronic security based on voice control, intelligent fireproofing, piped gas supply, centralised waste disposal and artificial intelligence-controlled electronic gazettes. This floor is modern, though in complete contrast with the ground and first floor of the house. The three floors have some interconnections. The way to the top floor is only through the staircase passing through the ground and first floor. You as an inhabitant enjoy living most of the time on the top floor, but you need to visit other floors as well.

What would be the experience of living in such a house that has three floors which are so radically different? This house becomes an incoherent motley of a cave-living and a modern smart home. The problem with such a house is that the newer items on the top floors do not seamlessly communicate with the older items on the ground floor. A new-age computer-controlled lighting system is very different from a lantern-based lighting system. They get into conflict most of the times. Even if some of the old items are redundant today, since they are all stored in the same house, they must sync up with each other however inefficient that process may be. The three floors are also interdependent structurally. The higher floors can't stand if the ground floor walls break down. Living in such a house and traversing through different floors could be a nightmare.

Welcome to the human brain! Structurally, it is very much like the house described above, just that the age difference of each layer of our brain is even more significant. Our brain has parts that came in existence at widely different points in time. While the old brain (also called reptilian brain) existed with the first humans millions of years ago, the newer cognitive brain called prefrontal cortex came into existence only a few thousand years ago. Even the development of different layers of the newer brain was hierarchical as they came up at different points in time during evolution. The old brain and new brain in each one of us are not necessarily in harmony with each other.

The reptilian brain includes the brain stem and cerebellum. The brain stem connects the brain to the spinal cord. Technically speaking, it consists of the medulla oblongata, pons and midbrain. The medulla oblongata controls our automatic body functions like blood pressure, breathing, body temperature, etc. Pons relays information relating to our sleep habits, eye movement, hearing, taste, etc., and midbrain controls our visual and auditory processing among many other things.

The next evolution of brain was our limbic system. They process some of our key functions like emotions and memory. It includes the amygdala, hippocampus and hypothalamus. Amygdala is known as the emotion centre and regulates emotions, while hippocampus helps in formation of memories. The hippocampus is embedded deep in the temporal lobe. Another important organ in this brain is the thalamus which is the centre for all sensory information. This layer sits on top of the brain stem and is also called mammalian brain.

The topmost layer is the new brain or the cortex. The cortex is the wrinkled grey matter at the topmost layer of our brain, just beneath the cranium. This is further divided into occipital lobe (primarily responsible for vision), temporal lobe (for auditory functions), parietal lobe (for sensory perception) and frontal lobe (responsible for expressing language). Prefrontal cortex (PFC), the newest part of the cortical brain, is the portion of brain where all higher-order cognitive functions happen. It acts as the CEO that does all the planning and controls their execution. I don't want to bore the readers with too many details on neuroanatomy. The point I was making is that our brain has a layered architecture with each layer evolving in different eras rather than being totally homogenous.

The mention of computer surfaces multiple times in the context of the human brain because it is the most sophisticated computational instrument we know today. Some people compare brain to the hardware of the computer and mind to the software. But in the case of the computer, the structure of hardware and software are distinct. For example, a software does not change the hardware of a computer. In the case of the human brain, however, the thoughts change the neural connections and eventually change the structure of the brain. So, the human brain has plasticity and there is no clear separation as in a computer. Also, there are huge differences in the way our brain stores, encodes and retrieves the information.

While the computer is faster in doing mathematical calculations, our brain has far more capacity to store and retrieve information called memory.

We have seen in the example of the house with three floors that unlike computers, different organs of the brains do not have the same 'manufacturing date'. On the other hand, all components of the computers like hard disk, RAM and keyboard have been created at the same time. Even if there were some differences in their manufacturing date, it would only be a few years. Hence, each component is tuned to the functioning of the other component. For example, the memory card has been tuned to the functioning of hard disk storage and the display monitor has been tuned to the internal processing. Each component is optimised in a way that the overall performance of the computer is optimal.

After looking at the layered architecture of our brain and understanding how it is different from the computer, let us look at how it creates so many conflicts in our daily existence.

Conflict 1: Emotive brain versus thinking brain

The key goal of our brain is to keep us alive. Our brain vigilantly scans the environment for threats all the time and is alarmed at even the smallest of suspicions. All our sensory organs be it eyes, ears or nose are always on the lookout for conditions that threaten our survival. While doing so, they overly focus on dangerous conditions and over amplify the negative signals.

The brain follows the principle of 'better safe than sorry'. Even if there is a 1 per cent chance that the animal hiding in the bush could be a lion, the limbic system alarms our sympathetic nervous system, the pituitary glands emit adrenaline, the blood circulation goes up, heartbeat increases, the body start sweating, and our legs get the command to run. There is little downside to this. At the worst, you might laugh at yourself when you discover later that the animal was a harmless cat and not a ferocious lion. Our old brain is programmed to amplify all the negative signals and produce an immediate emotional response to the same. In loose terms, we can say that our old brain has a strong negativity bias.

The reptilian brain behaves pretty much in the same way even in the case of animals. They look for prey and hunters and respond in a similar way. It is like automata. What makes humans different, is the development of the newer brain—the prefrontal cortex, or the part of the brain right behind our eyes. This is the thinking brain; it does not work on automatic reflexes like the emotive brain. This is where we plan things in advance and execute them.

This part of the brain defines logic, reasoning and our personality. It can also override the inputs of the emotive brain, if trained suitably. Had this prefrontal cortex not developed in humans, we would pretty much have been like animals. The executive brain frees us from the compulsion of our encoded biology and makes us people of different temperaments.

During the hunter-gatherer days, human lives were full of threats. We could not even sleep peacefully. Any animal could attack us any moment and make us its sumptuous meal. Our existence was like walking on a tightrope. This made our old brain extra sensitive towards the threats. It could easily get triggered and evoke a response of fight or flight. One of the strongest emotions we possess is 'fear'. It made evolutionary sense in those days.

In modern-day life, we do not face a threat to our lives as much as we faced during cave-dwelling days. We live in well-built houses with all modern amenities to guard against any life-threatening incidents. We have good medical facilities in case we fall ill. Though we have newer kind of threats, the overall safety has increased by order of magnitude. This is known to our analytical new brain, but the old reptilian brain continues to operate in the same way.

All of us have experienced it in our daily lives. The 'flight or fight' response get triggered very often even when it is completely unnecessary. We worry not about the prevailing threat but invent future worries. These threats are no longer only physical threats but even something like social embarrassment. We easily get panicked. When we get panicked, the first thing that happens in our brain is that the amygdala takes over the emotional response of anger. Even while our analytical brain suggests relaxing, the old brain triggers the survival button. At this time, the prefrontal cortex is practically shut down. Our survival biology takes over. Many times, when we think back, we realise that our response was not appropriate.

The impact of triggering the 'fight or flight' response too often is not trivial. All the hormones released in the body stay for quite some time. Since the body prepares itself for an impending crisis which is non-existent, it results in other aggressive behaviour. Anger is one of them. Anger is a self-defence mechanism which is triggered by the old brain by overruling the new brain. We never behave rationally when we are angry. We repent later, but on the spur of the moment it is difficult to control our behaviour. Essentially, we are caught between the fight between the old and new brain.

Conflict 2: Conscious and subconscious brain

The conscious brain is something that gets into our awareness and is under our control. We have direct access to it. The subconscious brain on the contrary, is not under our direct control even though it controls most of the important functions of the body. For example, under normal circumstances, we do not worry about our blood circulation, breath control or the digestive system in our body. And thank God that we don't have to do it—the subconscious brain does it for us. It is also the most energy efficient part and does things smoothly compared to the conscious brain that consumes most of our energy.

Joseph Murphy in his book *The Power of Your Subconscious Mind,* says that when we pray to God, we appeal to our subconscious mind to act in accordance with our desires. The power of the subconscious mind makes it happen by aligning our overall effort and channelising it in the right direction. It is eventually we ourselves who work towards fulfilling those desires. This is how prayer works.

Sigmund Freud explained the unconscious and conscious mind in the form of Id, Ego and Superego. Id according to Freud is the primitive unconscious instinct that consists of hidden memories, sexual desires, and aggression. Superego is the moral values that one learns from society or parents. Ego is the mediator between the desires of Id and the Superego. Freud's theory of psychoanalysis was based on this conflict of Id, Ego and Superego. Though most of the

Freudian theories have been rejected by modern psychologists, it still brings out the conflicts of conscious and subconscious minds.

Conflict 3: The noisy chatterbox

Even within the new brain, things are not that harmonious. You can observe how our thoughts jump from one subject to another at random. The brain gets signals from different senses like eyes, ears, nose, skin, etc., and combines all of them to construct a reality. While doing so, it mixes it with memories and emotions that are stored in our brain. The brain can generate thoughts even without any external sensors purely by using imagination. The result is a chaotic blend of thoughts and feelings. We often say that the world is chaotic, but our inner world is as chaotic if not more. At any moment, there are numerous conversations going on in our mind; luckily our attention is like a spotlight that focuses on some and we are aware of only those thoughts.

With so many chaotic conversations going on in our mind, it is a wonder we don't go mad.

It seems the brain has a unique ability to distinguish brain chatter from external world conversations. For example, the brain knows well if some words are spoken by the person standing in front of you or if they are generated by your own brain. Then you apply your rationality to act in the most appropriate way. In some clinical cases (schizophrenia for example), the ability of the brain to distinguish between the two vanishes. So, the thought of talking to a person will appear as the real person talking to you. Schizophrenics suffer from hallucinations too. That is why some of these patients turn delusional and they may talk to imaginary persons. They appear to be talking to themselves, but to their brain, they are talking to real people. I understand it is a very complicated situation and any simplistic explanation like this does not do justice in explaining this situation, but the point was to highlight that our brain is full of chaotic chatter. Thank God we have a way to deal with it so that we don't turn mad.

One theory about the bigger size of our brain is that it grew not because of the analytical demands but because of our gossiping nature. Our brain is constantly busy in what others think of us or what others think of others. It mixes fact, fiction and imagination, and in doing so, our brain is telling us stories all the time; it is constantly at work.

Conflict 4: Right brain versus left brain

Another interesting aspect of the brain conundrum is known as left brain and right brain division. Our brain is structurally divided into two parts by an imaginary vertical plane running through the middle of our two eyes. It has been said in popular literature that some people who are analytical, logical, etc., use their left brain predominantly while the ones who are more creative use their right brain. There is no scientific evidence to support this hypothesis. Both the hemispheres of the brains are interconnected by a bundle of fibres called corpus callosum that transmits messages from one side to the other. Most of the cognitive functions are equally distributed across both hemispheres. However, there are some localisations of functions like language in the left hemisphere. Another interesting aspect of the brain anatomy is that the right hemisphere receives sensory input and directs movement on the left side of the body and vice versa.

The interconnection of the two hemispheres of the brain keeps all the information in sync. But what happens when this interconnection gets severed, and our two hemispheres get disconnected? Does our consciousness get divided into two?

Incidentally, this aspect has been studied in patients suffering from chronic seizures whose corpus callosum was surgically cut to cure them. The two hemispheres in their brains were not talking to each other. When these patients were shown objects that their right eye (and hence the left brain) saw, they could correctly identify and name the object. Now when the same object was shown to their left eye, which was processed by the right brain, the patient could not name the object. This is understandable because the language capabilities and object identification is primarily localised in the left brain.

A more interesting observation was how the left brain tried to invent a fictitious story to describe the object while it got no input from the right brain. The right brain saw the object while the left brain was forced to describe something that it did not see (as the interconnection was severed). The funny thing is during these experiments, the patient did not say that he or she did not see an object but tried to invent a fabricated story. This was a fascinating observation on how our sense of self is driven by the dynamic interactions of the different hemispheres in our brain. There are instances of such split-brain patients where the left hand (controlled by right brain) starts acting of its own as if it was some alien object. Michio Kaku in his book *The Future of the Mind*, says that: -

"There is one documented case in which a man was about to hug his wife with one hand, only to find that the other hand had an entirely different agenda. It delivered a right hook to her face. Another woman reported that she would pick out a dress with one hand, only to see her other hand grab an entirely different outfit. Meanwhile, one man had difficulty sleeping at night thinking that his other rebellious hand might strangle him."

Essentially emotive and thinking brain, conscious and subconscious brain, left and right brain do contradict each other. This is what we call war within our brain. It is not a homogenous, synchronised and harmonious organ but a chaotic and noisy marketplace where everyone is craving for attention. Our brain chatter never stops, not even when we sleep. In fact, the brain activity comes down only by 10–15 per cent during our sleep. This means our brain is continuously at work; when it stops, we die. Unlike the computer, it never shuts down, it never restarts. Since the date of its coming into existence till the end of it, our brain is continuously working.

Today, when we are building intelligent AI machines like a self-driving car, do we ever want to replicate something like the human brain? Something that is so conflicted and imperfect?

Most scientists believe that just as modern flights have little resemblance to birds, the future AI brains will have little resemblance to human brains. Human brains have engineering imperfections as we understand more about it. It is ironical, however, that one day we plan to create a perfect artificial brain using our imperfect human brain.

Key Learnings:

1. Our brain has evolved over a long period of time and different organs within the brain have different ages. Our brain is like a city that has some very old structures and some new-age glass buildings.

2. Our old brain is something that we share with animals that manages all our internal body functions like blood circulation, food digestion, etc.

3. The old brain has a strong negativity bias to keep us extra safe. Even if there is a remote chance of an animal hiding in the bush being a tiger, our brain triggers a fight or flight response.

4. The limbic system consists of organs that trigger a strong emotional response like fear (fight or flight).

5. Our new brain (prefrontal cortex) provides us with the analytical capability, planning, executing and all cognitive functions as we know is unique to us humans.

6. The old and new brain are at conflict in many situations (extra sensitivity to external threat for example). The strong emotional response by the old brain shuts off the analytical

abilities of the new brain. That is why we are more prone to make mistakes when we are angry.

7. Even within the analytical new brain, our thoughts are never synchronised. Our internal brain chatter is like a chaotic marketplace. Luckily, we have the awareness to differentiate that from real-world events and we preserve our sanity.

8. We have a conscious brain that gets into our awareness while we are oblivious to the subconscious brain. The subconscious brain is very efficient and aligning the energy of this brain can help us achieve great success.

9. Another division of the brain is left hemisphere versus the right one. It is said in popular literature (though there is little scientific support), that the left brain is analytical while the right brain is creative.

10. Our brain consists of organs that are at war with each other most of the times. It is an imperfect computer. It is an open question if the scientists would ever like to recreate something like this when venturing into artificial intelligence.

Master of Fate

It matters not how strait the gate,
How charged with punishments the scroll,
*I am the **master of my fate**,*
*I am the **captain of my soul.***

—William Ernest Henley

Do we have a choice in what we become?

Paulo Coelho in his book *Alchemist,* describes the story of a young shepherd named Santiago. The shepherd is a humble boy who is content with his life; his desires are very few. He wants to roam around the place with his sheep, drink wine and read books. Then one day he suddenly gets a wild dream—of hidden treasure in Africa. He sells his sheep and embarks on an unknown journey full of hazards and surprises. He follows his heart to realise what the author calls his 'Personal Legend'. One of the most quotable quotes in the book goes like 'when you want something, all the universe conspires in helping you to achieve it'. Though the book is a fictional account set in ancient times, it is quoted in many leadership sessions as a supporting argument of human will power.

Let me quote another equally interesting book, *Outliers* by Malcolm Gladwell. The author analyses the list of most successful hockey players in the Canadian national league. An apparent inference about these players could be that they achieved their success due to hard work and talent. After all, no one is a born hockey player, one must learn it. On analysing the players' list, he shares a startling fact— majority of them were born in January. Digging further, the author discovers that these students were selected not because they were the best but because they were the oldest in the selection age group. The junior hockey team selection age cut-off was 1 January, so a child born on 2–31 January had a natural advantage of one year of physical growth compared to his peers born in December. During early childhood years, a one-year head start is a huge advantage in physical development. Early selection and training in good clubs gave them further cumulative advantage and they ended up being at the top of the league. The author concludes that in this setup, whether a child can grow to be a successful hockey player depends less on his skill and training and more on the month of the year he was born. One has hardly any control on which month of the year one is born. *Outliers* brings up several such examples—the essence of which is, we hardly have control over what we become. It is either the circumstances, our genes or both responsible for what we call our destiny. It is a feel-good argument in case we believe that we could not be as successful in our life as we had wanted to be—after all it was our fate that failed us.

The two authors make contrary arguments, and both of them are valid. A more pertinent point to discuss could be how much we are alike and how much we are different from each other.

Biologically, all humans are pretty much alike. 97 per cent of our genes are common and can be traced back to similar ancestry. This is the reason that we all have a similar physical structure with two hands, two legs, two eyes, etc. We may differ a bit in skin complexion, body weight, height or facial features, but the differences are insignificant compared to the commonalities. Behaviourally also, we have more similarities than differences—we all laugh in a certain way, raise our voices when we get angry and show similar emotions. Though we may speak different languages, there are major similarities that are impossible to ignore. The evolutionary biology is primarily the study of these commonalities. Physically, our selfish genes in each of us are only marginally different in height, weight, complexion, etc. The role of DNA in our physical development is well established now. With genome mapping today, a lot of predictions can be made about the physical development.

While the variability in the physical aspects of humans is limited, the variability in the cognitive abilities is far more significant. We know how one person becomes a genius whereas another person (and most of us) end up being an average Joe. We can safely conclude that all of us have the same underlying asset (presuming that our brain is the common hardware), but we differ in our abilities and willingness to optimally leverage that asset. As a result, we are 7+ billion unique minds and all of them are completely different from each other. If we had a tool to accurately map the human brain, we would have known that in the limited matter of 1.5 kg of brain mass, our neuron wirings are immensely unique and infinitely different from each other. Even though we have similar bodies and a common brain architecture, at the level of minds we are all different.

Thanks to this variability, it is easy to create a personality blueprint that is unique to any individual. We all think differently and react differently to the same situation. We have a different mental model of the world and we interpret the same conditions differently. We may be two individuals born in the same family, provided similar upbringing and exposure but soon enough, we develop uniqueness in behaviour and thinking. This is really a miracle and it makes the world an interesting place for humans. How boring this world would have been, had all of us thought in exactly the same way, had similar feelings, and reacted in the similar manner. We would have been no different from inanimate things like tables and chairs.

One of the most contested debates of all time has been—nature versus nurture. Are we born intelligent, or do we become intelligent due to the environment and our own efforts?

Our physical body is pretty much governed by our DNA, just as for any other species. Each cell of the body contains unique information that eventually develop into our specific height, colour, body structure, etc. Most of these characteristics we inherit, and that is why we look so much like our parents. In some cases, twins are indistinguishable in appearance from each other. Humans have evolved possibly from apes and their body structures have developed further. But these evolutions are very slow changes that happen across several generations. They are affected over a long period of time in what Charles Darwin calls 'natural law of selection'. There is a huge amount of information that is encoded in our biology.

There could be some variations in our physical structures as well. Based on how we groom our body, one of the twins can be a long-distance runner while the other could turn out to be a couch potato with an oversized belly. We can change the size and shape of our muscles based on the workouts and activities we do. Our lifestyle can influence our ability to stay healthy or increase our propensity for diseases. Essentially, some part of our biology can be altered while most of them can't be altered. In case of our physical body, the debate is settled; we are predominantly a product of our biology. We can't do much about that. Same is true for animals also— whatever it tries, a cat will never grow into a lion.

How about the brain development? Is it just like the development of any other organ of the body? What is the contribution of nature versus nurture in this case?

Of all the animals on this planet, humans have the longest developmental period from birth to adulthood. A calf can stand up on its feet just a few hours after birth and start running, a baby bird can start flying in just a few weeks, a new-born turtle can crawl into the sea soon after hatching, and so on. But talk of a human being and it takes several years of caregiving and parenting. Raising a child is probably the most time-consuming and exhausting exercise for humans. Historians believe that one of the reasons that marriage evolved as a common institution in all civilisations is precisely this—the offspring have a greater chance of survival in such a setup. Two parents can take care of the kids far better than a single parent. It is just not providing enough food for growth but teaching them languages to communicate, handholding them and helping them acquire knowledge of this world for their survival. For animals—they don't have to worry about anything beyond procreation. The offspring take care of themselves without much support. For humans, this is such an exhausting and time-consuming activity that it takes up half of our lifetimes.

But this long period of development has a positive side as well. This allows the developmental brain to adjust to the environment more easily. A child born in Japan can learn Japanese during this time while someone born in France may speak French fluently. The human brain can adapt to the surroundings more easily during this period. It can learn new skills, language and sports.

Our brain is only 2 per cent of our body weight but consumes 25 per cent of the energy produce. During the development period, this even goes higher than 50 per cent. One of the reasons that the babies sleep a lot is precisely this—their brain is growing fast and needs a lot more energy. The developmental needs of the brain are so high during childhood that it delays the development of the other body parts.

Early scientists believed that unlike other parts of the body, the human brain was not composed of discrete cells. The early pictures of the brain looked enmeshed with multiple cross connections, so the early theory of the brain in 1871 by Joseph Von Gerlach proposed that brains do not have discrete cells; rather it is a single continuous network of cells. Subsequently, Camillo Golgi used the staining technique to picturise the neurons, but he also came to the same conclusion that the brain is a single continuous network of cells. This came to be known as 'reticular theory of brain'.

In 1888, Santiago Ramon Y Cajal used the same technique of Golgi, but he arrived at a completely different conclusion, i.e., the neurons are discrete cells that are interconnected with each other. This theory came to be known as 'neuron doctrine' which contradicted the 'reticular theory'. The debate was finally settled in 1950 when the electron microscope observed that there were some gaps between two neurons that is known as synapses. So, it led to the conclusion that neurons were indeed discrete cells. The discovery of synapses was the magical moment in the brain science history.

Now the neurologists understand and have traced the brain development from childhood. It is estimated that there are about 100 billion neurons in an adult brain. These neurons vary in length from a few millimetres to more than a metre. Each neuron is connected, sometimes up to 10,000 other neurons through synapses. The neurons communicate with each other though electric signals. A neuron possesses many root-like extensions called dendrites. They receive chemical impulses from other neurons. They are converted to electrical impulses. If the electrical impulses are large enough, they are transmitted to the cell body. The axon carries the electrical signals from the cell body to the axon terminals, which then passes the impulse to another neuron. Neurons are connected by synapses. The information is transmitted by chemicals called neurotransmitters. Neurotransmitters cross the synapse and bind to the receptors on the dendrites on the other neuron.

This is how neurotransmission works. It works the same way in each one of our brains. The mystery is not in the neurons, the mystery is in the way these neurons are interconnected. That is where we all differ from each other. In other words, we are all wired differently and uniquely.

How Do These Networks in the Brain Evolve? Is There a Pattern in the Development of These Networks?

When the child is still in the womb, the neurons start developing and connecting with each other in the creation of predefined pathways. Humans have maximum number of neurons during the early days of childhood. Since these neurons are all connected to each other like one giant web, this is not of much use. As the child grows, the neuron connections start following certain patterns based on either genetic (nature) disposition or environmental factors (nurture). Some synapses get strengthened while some gets dissolved. This process of neuron regrouping is called 'pruning'. It is for this reason that we can learn a new language fast as a child while we struggle to do the same as an adult or we pick up an awkward accent when we learn. It is for this reason that a child can learn swimming much faster than adults. There is a window of opportunity when all of us must learn new things.

As a child, our brain is highly dynamic and shapes into a different mould based on the genetic and environmental factors. There was a long-held belief that once we grow to be an adult, our brain matures, and it becomes more rigid as it loses its plasticity. Probably that could have been the basis of the proverb—*'an old dog can't learn new tricks'*. Subsequent scientific experiments, however, have proved this hypothesis wrong. The brain structures continue to change till we die, though the extent of plasticity may come down. As you are reading this book, your brain is re-wiring itself and forming new connections, strengthening some while diminishing some. In the medical science it is called 'neuroplasticity'.

The neuroplasticity is the Holy Grail of learning for humans. This gives us the immense brain power that we can acquire during our lifetime. We need not be entirely dependent upon our genes for this. If we can control our thoughts and actions, we can re-wire our brains the way we want. This is also the scientific basis of the proverbial saying that 'we become what we think'. Thoughts have a real existence, and they change our brain structure. If we worry about certain things quite often—our brain strengthens the 'worry pathway' that makes us even more worried. On the other hand, if we often think positively, our brain makes it look more so. This is what the psychologist call 'will power'. If we decide to do certain things, practice it for a few days and stick to the rituals by repeating it, our re-wired brain will make sure that it becomes as effortless as possible. This is what author Robin Sharma means when he introduces the concept of the 21 days rule to form a habit in his motivational book, *A Monk Who Sold His Ferrari*. Neuroplasticity is the underlying scientific reason behind this observed behaviour. Our neural wirings change and that is how we learn new things by repetitions.

So, if you want to be a genius, you must first believe that you can be a genius. By repeated thinking and autosuggestions (and of course acting on a plan), the brain will re-wire itself to make you a genius. This looks like an over-simplistic explanation but there have been experiments conducted to prove this point.

> In one controlled experiment, several knee patients were scheduled for knee surgery. While some of them were operated upon and their joint problems were fixed, for some of them it was purposely not fixed during the surgery. The patients of both groups were told that their knee problems had been fixed. Surprisingly, the patients of both the groups reported that their knee problem had vanished. This is called placebo effect and is routinely exercised to understand the impact of new medicines.

There is also a converse of such experiments where a patient constantly thinks (more of an illusion) that he has caught a certain disease till the brain re-wires itself to create the illness. This is called nocebo effect. The hypnosis works in the same way—the subject is made to believe by repeated reinforcements so that the brain really starts seeing that as reality. The point made here is that the constant thought can change the brain structure in a way that we think.

Psychologists explain that repeated behaviour becomes your habit which is difficult to change. In other words, your behaviour shapes up your brain that reinforces that behaviour. So if you lie too many times, your brain structure changes and that forces you to be a compulsive liar and you can't escape from that. This also explains why old habits die hard. It is no longer our wish—it becomes our compulsion.

There are differences between what the psychologists call 'growth mindset' and 'fixed mindset'. It is easy to talk about 'fixed mindset'. All of us have certain inherent capabilities that we call talent. We perform according to our talents that are different for different people. Some of us are blessed to be a born genius with those capabilities. This is an easy but fatalist justification of why we can't achieve things that successful people do.

A 'growth mindset' person believes that he can alter his behaviour to achieve the things that he wants. Such people believe that we can become the person we want to be. Napoleon Hill wrote a book, *Think and Grow Rich*, way back in 1937 that captures this aspect well. According to him, thoughts are things. The thoughts have real existence. If you can understand your thoughts and guide them—you can make your dreams come true. Buddha is believed to have said, "What you think you become." All that you need to do is, to train your mind. A genius is no different from an average Joe, other than this aspect of mind control.

If all of us know that a trained mind is a genius mind, why all of us don't go for it. The answer is—it is not easy and requires years of practice. Spiritual master, Sadhguru explains that with an example in his book *Inner Engineering*.

> *In ancient India, there was a saint who was known to do miraculous things like living without food for months, even domesticate most dangerous animals in the jungle and treat terminally sick people. Some people believed that he could even walk on water. He was revered by common people more like God.*
>
> *Once, a young monk approached the saint and asked him the secret of his greatness. The saint*

replied plainly—it is mastery of your own thoughts and mind.

The young monk insisted that the saint must teach him how to master the mind. The saint replied that it required a lot of practice, but the young monk persisted. The saint finally relented. He told him, "Come to this riverbank every day very early in the morning, sit in mediation for an hour and repeat a thousand times that you want to achieve the miraculous power of mind. Do this for six months without fail and you will achieve that you want."

The young monk could not believe it. But he had full faith in the saint so decided to practice the same.

"By the way when you meditate, don't think of monkeys," said the saint before the monk left.

After three months, the young monk met the saint again.

"What happened?" asked the saint. "Have you been following the mediation as I said?"

"Master, as soon as I start meditating and think not to think of monkeys, I see monkeys in my head all over. I just can't get rid of them. Even during the day, my head is full of monkeys. I don't want to attain your mystic power to do miracles, please get rid of these monkeys in my head," replied the young monk.

This fable captures the dilemma of the power of mind versus power to control it. Who controls what—does the mind control us, or do we control the mind?

Philosophers and gurus have written voluminous texts on the importance of mind and the need to train it. A trained mind works according to the goals given to it. These goals can appear impossible to achieve in the beginning, but with persistence the mind self-organises itself to create a conducive environment. This is the characteristic of a growth mindset. Greatness is a habit cultivated by genius. It is true that our mind controls us, but we can train our mind bit by bit to respond in a certain way. It is said that our thoughts make up our behaviour, our behaviour makes up our habit, our habits make us our character, and finally our character makes up our thought. It is a circular reference at each stage. We become what we think, and we think what we become.

From the neuroscience perspective, the growth mindset can be proven empirically. Our brain can learn any behaviour and acquire knowledge if exposed suitably. Our brain is a mesh of neurons—billions of them connected to thousands of each other. These interconnections represent our memories, skills and cognitive abilities. The strength of these connections is something that determines the neural pathways.

The synapses follow a very simple principle—'neurons that fire together, wire together'. So, if we do certain things repeatedly, our brain learns it and creates neural pathways that results in kind of automating that activity. That results in the trained mind.

There is another aspect of neural phenomenon—'use it or lose it'. If we do not use certain skills that we have, it will weaken the neural connections and over a period of time, we can lose that skill. So essentially it means that with our self-belief and efforts, we can become the person we want to be.

If there was a genius ever born on this planet, many of us would say it was Einstein. His name has become an adjective for intellect. There is an interesting story about his brain after he died (there is even a documentary made on this). Einstein's wish was to be cremated, but the pathologist, Dr Harvey on duty thought it would be a shame to destroy a brain like that. Dr Harvey who conducted the post-mortem of Einstein, secretly hid the brain hoping to discover the secret of being a genius. He cut the brain into 240 blocks and made a thousand slices out of it. Later, he sent the brain pieces to various researchers in different universities.

Michio Kaku who wrote the book *Einstein's Cosmos,* says though there were some minor anomalies in Einstein's brain (a certain part of the brain called angular gyrus was larger and the inferior parietal region of both the hemispheres were 15 per cent wider than the average), his brain was, in fact, smaller than the normal human brain. The genius did not lie in his brain. He goes on to say that Einstein was a genius because he was passionately curious and kept his focus. From the age of sixteen to twenty-six, Einstein focused on the problem of light and this led to special relativity theory. For the next ten years, he focused on the theory of gravity that gave us the black holes and big bang theory. From the age of thirty-six to the end of his life, he focused on the theory of everything. He was reportedly weak in mathematics in his schooldays. So, the genius of Einstein did not lie in his extraordinary brain but in his remarkable ability to conduct thought experiments which in all probability was inculcated by him.

We can be the captain of our ship and the master of our soul. This is very well captured in the motivational poem of Walter D Wintle:

> *If you think you are beaten, you are*
> *If you think you dare not, you don't,*
> *If you like to win, but you think you can't*
> *It is almost certain you won't.*
>
> *If you think you'll lose, you're lost*
> *For out of the world we find,*

Success begins with a fellow's will
It's all in the state of mind.

If you think you are outclassed, you are
You've got to think high to rise,
You've got to be sure of yourself before
You can ever win a prize.

Life's battles don't always go
To the stronger or faster man,
But soon or late the man who wins
Is the man WHO THINKS HE CAN!

Key Takeaway Points:

1. Our biological properties are largely encoded in our DNA that we inherit from our parents. Our physical attributes are largely governed by inheritance and there is very little intervention we can make.

2. While we are very similar to each other in physical development, we are infinitely different when it comes to our mind. We are 7+ billion different individuals, not because of our bodies but our minds.

3. At the individual neuron level, we all are still the same. The magic of the mind does not happen due to individual neurons but their interconnections. It is the wiring of neurons in our brains that make us so different.

4. Humans have one of the longest development periods (birth to adulthood) among all species. The reason behind that could be a long cycle of brain development. The human brain consumes most of the energy (up to 50 per cent) during this phase, slowing down the growth of other body parts.

5. This long developmental period, however, helps us in extensive brain evolution compared to animals. We learn languages, acquire knowledge, and learn skills to adapt to different environments.

6. As a child, we have a window of opportunity when we can learn new skills easily. This is the period when the neural connections are getting created in children. It is for this reason that a child can learn swimming faster than an adult.

7. Just like our bodies, nature and nurture both play important roles in the development of our brain. Our DNA contains the information about our body as well as the brain. However, in case of the mind, it is we who play a significant role in development.

8. Our brain has a unique ability to change and reorganise itself based on our thoughts and

actions. This 'neuroplasticity' provides us with an opportunity to learn things throughout our lifetime.

9. Our brain follows a simple principle, 'neurons that wire together, fire together'. If we repeat certain thoughts and acts, it eventually becomes our habit and changes the brain structure.

10. We can train our brain and achieve self-mastery by our own efforts. Thanks to our cognitive brain, we are not limited by our biology and we can strive to achieve any goal.

Language—Cognitive Revolution of Mind

A language is not just words. It's a culture, a tradition, a unification of a community, a whole history that creates what a community is. It's all embodied in a language.

—*Noam Chomsky*

In the cognitive evolution of mankind, if there is one most significant milestone, then it is the evolution of language. Human beings are intelligent because we can think, but can we think without language? Some experiments suggest that our brain can think using images and symbols as well, but its ability is quite limited. Most importantly, language is used for communication, that aligns the thought process of all humans. Using language, we can add up our intellectual prowess to achieve things that could have been unachievable. Human civilisation would cease to exist in its current form if it were not for languages.

Just imagine if the monkeys could talk to each other just like humans do, there is no reason they would not have been as intelligent as anyone of us. They could have created their own community and elected representatives to fight for their monkey-rights. They could have raised their own army and limited humans who commit atrocities on them. Many animals have limited sound-producing abilities but nowhere near to humans who can produce such a sophisticated and rich variety of sounds. It is not evident why such higher-order language skills could develop only in humans and not in any other mammals. Language is a uniquely human phenomenon, rather something that makes us human.

There is no clear evidence or agreement among experts on when this language skill emerged in humans—it happened possibly several thousand years before. How it emerged is also a mystery. Noam Chomsky, the noted linguist, believes that the language was passed on directly from God to a single individual. This later spread to one another. Even Sanskrit, possibly one of the oldest languages dated 5,000 BC, is called *Deva vani*—language of the gods. It is believed that language was invented and later passed on to humans in its purest form. In scientific terms, it can be explained as a chance mutation that happened in certain individuals. This mutation later progressed to the next generation as natural selection. Of course, Charles Darwin would never approve of any such abrupt developmental theory. It also does not explain why such a chance mutation happened only in humans and not apes.

A more commonly accepted theory of language is that it possibly evolved slowly over a long period of time. Humans became bipedal and started walking on their two legs which freed up their hands for other activities. They started to communicate using hand gestures. This slowly moved to the face with organs like the eyes and mouth participating actively (hence the term expression) and later got localised to the mouth. They started associating familiar sounds with certain objects and later accorded meaning to them. The next step of evolution was associating arbitrary sounds to objects and ideas.

This was a great evolution even from a physical perspective because it freed up the hands for other miscellaneous work. Human development leapfrogged both from the cognitive and biological perspective. In the somatosensory map of our cortex, mouth is represented by the largest area denoting a large patch of neurons dedicated to the muscle movements in our mouth. We can move our lips and tongues in a wide variety of ways to create new sounds not available in any other natural form. Our vocal apparatus of the mouth is the most evolved among all living species.

Experiments with Language Deprivation

To know whether language abilities are innate in humans or learnt while growing up, a few experiments have been conducted in the distant past. In modern times, such an experiment will be devastating for the child. American literary scholar Roger Shattuck called this a 'Forbidden Experiment'. This essentially requires isolating an infant from the normal use of spoken or signed language. Although the scientific outcome of such an experiment can be fascinating, it would be extremely unethical. Fictional literature has exploited this to the full imagination—there is a specific name given to such a child—'feral child'. Moreover, a character like Mowgli has been very popular.

Records of forbidden experiment can be found as early as 440 BC in *Herodotus Histories*. An Egyptian Pharaoh subjected a child to language deprivation and concluded that the Phrygian race must have predated Egyptians because the first word the child said after the long deprivation was *bekos* meaning bread in Phrygian. This experiment was debunked by historians and linguists though, as it could just be a babbling.

Another experiment was done by James IV of Scotland in the 15th century. Two children were raised by a mute woman on an isolated island in Scotland. It was alleged that the children spoke good Hebrew, but historians were sceptical of such a finding. Several centuries later, a similar experiment was done by Akbar during the Mughal period in India. The emperor concluded that speech resulted from hearing language, and those raised without hearing human voices could grow to be mute. This conclusion is more plausible and better accepted in the scientific community.

A normal human today has a huge vocabulary of close to 100,000 plus words, while we use less than a few thousand words for day-to-day work. Why do we learn so many words if we don't intend to use them (excluding those who do this for their exams)?

A speculation on the theory of this richness of human vocabulary is that language evolved as a tool for courtship mainly for sexual selection. Literature and music essentially were prized skills that got rewarded in the sexual selection. Richness of vocabulary is also a measure of intelligence.

There are close to 5,000 major languages in the world today. Any child can easily learn one or more languages during the early growth days. However, it becomes difficult to learn a new language for adults.

It possibly indicates that language ability is closely linked with the evolution of physical brain areas during early development. This is known as the critical period hypothesis which means that learning of language is linked to age. There is an ideal time to learn a language after which it becomes difficult. It is for this reason that most people are proficient in their mother tongue but are never able to attain the same level of proficiency even after several years of practice. Even when we can learn a new language later as an adult, we develop unnatural accents. We can easily make out a French speaking English or a German speaking Chinese. Some sounds if not learnt early enough in childhood are difficult to produce during the rest of our lives. Language crossover is very difficult for grown-ups.

This also explains why the colonisers tried to impose their own language over the people they ruled. Language is a strong tool for domination. The native speakers have an inherent advantage driven by brain development during early stage, while those who learn later have a natural disadvantage. The first thing the colonisers did was to hire in the administration, people who only knew their master's language and not the local language. The locals were forced to learn the new language to communicate with the state. Since language is also linked with intelligence and creativity—a forced language can seriously impede an individual's ability. It has been proven that IQ test in an alternate language (other than the mother tongue), brings the IQ score down by several points. Education of a child in the mother tongue has been proven to create higher level of knowledge and skills.

Language also encapsulates what we call culture. The customs, ideas and behaviour are intricately tagged with the language. That is why we see that exact translations between languages are so difficult because the ideas and concepts represented by different languages are different. There is no one-to-one match. It is for this reason that people are so passionate about their mother tongues. History is replete with examples where people have fought wars for the supremacy of their language. At the same time, it has also united people speaking the same language.

Even today, language processing is one of the toughest areas for artificial intelligence. The way humans learn and produce language is the topmost form of creativity. Semantics is far more complex than arithmetic operations. It will be fair to say if there was no language, there would be no knowledge.

Language from Neuroscience Perspective

Now, we understand that human brains have specific areas to handle languages. There are two areas that we currently know which are called Broca's area and Wernicke's area. Broca's area is responsible for speech production while the Wernicke's area is responsible for semantics or comprehension of speech. Both are located on the left side of the brain and are interconnected.

In case of lesions in the Broca's area (named after its inventor) the person has difficulty in speech production. They may face difficulty in forming complete sentences, they may omit verbs, pronouns, etc. For example, a patient who wants to say that he has a smart son who goes to university might end up saying—'Son...university...smart...boy'. In rare cases, the patient may just repeat one word. Broca had a patient who could only pronounce 'Tan'; hence he was nicknamed Tan. Tan had a lesion in the Broca's area.

Another type of aphasia (Wernicke's) is when the patient has no problem in speaking, (speech motor control is alright) but has difficulty in comprehending, i.e., not able to get the semantics or the meaning of what he says. A person suffering from this aphasia might say something like

'I called my mother on television and did not understand the door. It was too breakfast, but they came from far to near. My mother is not too old for me to be young'.

These sentences may be correct grammatically while they may not mean anything. The patient may well be aware, but they can't help it due to the damage to their Wernicke's area. The above example might be the extreme case where we can say, 'the person does not talk sense'.

A third form of aphasia called conduction aphasia occurs when the patient is unable to repeat speech. They can understand sentences, they can speak sentences but can't repeat them. This is due to the problem in the interconnection between Broca's and Wernicke's area.

With all the above forms of aphasia, it is evident that the evolution of language is directly mapped with our brains.

Key Takeaway Points:

1. Language is the most important milestone in the journey of human cognition. It is probably the single most reason humans evolved so rapidly compared to their other living peers.

2. It is not known for sure when the linguistic skills developed in humans. Perhaps it

happened millions of years ago, specifically in humans, as no other species seem to have this skill beyond some limited forms of sounds. Even our nearest relatives, apes could not be trained in languages after years of efforts.

3. How the language skill developed is also unclear. Perhaps, it evolved as a replacement of hand gestures, first in the form of related sounds and then arbitrary sounds to denote specific objects and ideas.

4. Many people believe that the first language was created by God and transferred to humans. In evolutionary terms, it can be explained as a chance mutation in our genes that got carried further in newer generations.

5. Language is also linked with the intelligence. An average adult has a vocabulary of 100,000+ words, while he or she may use only a few thousands in their day-to-day lives.

6. Any language deprivation experiment on humans (children) is considered so debilitating that it is called a forbidden experiment in modern times. Popular literature sometimes refers to such a child as a 'feral child'. These are the children who have lived in jungles among animals without any human influence.

7. Some of the earlier experiments proved that if the child is not exposed to language during early development, it may well turn out to be mute and deaf.

8. Now we understand that there are specific brain areas in humans responsible for language. Broca's area is responsible for speech production while Wernicke's area is responsible for semantics.

9. Lesions in the language processing part of the brain can affect the language abilities in human. It can result in incorrect sentences to sometimes speaking grammatically correct sentences without any meaning.

10. The language development is strictly linked to early brain development. There is an ideal age to learn a new language after which it becomes difficult. This is known as the critical period hypothesis.

Are We Really Free?

You say: I am not free. But I have raised and lowered my arm. Everyone understands that this illogical answer is an irrefutable proof of freedom.

—Leo Tolstoy

When you throw a stone at a street dog, you pretty much know how it will react. Either it will charge at you (in that case you will repent the act) or run away from the place. Well, there is a third possibility of it coming back after a few minutes with all their brethren in the street to attack you, but the possibility of the same is very rare. We can say this for all other animals as well—we can predict their behaviour for any stimulus. The reaction strictly follows the stated action. The biological rule is very simple —if the attacked animal is stronger than the attacking one, it will fight back, else it will run away from that scene.

That is why animals are called 'automata'—there are few possibilities between action and reaction. They don't have choices over their actions. They are programmed biologically to react in a specific way. In essence, they lack free will. Thankfully, it is for this precise reason they can't be tried in any court of law. Even if they were, they would have just argued that they have no control over their actions. So if anything, it is their biology that should be blamed and punished, not them. They can't commit crime. There is no concept of an evil dog or a criminal cat.

Humans on the other hand are different in this aspect. They are presumed to possess 'free will', i.e., ability to choose their actions from infinite possibilities. They also can predict the outcome of their actions—called consequences. For this reason, they are called rational beings—different from automata. When you hit a man (you may choose not to do this experiment though)—you very well know that he can avenge himself in a thousand ways that may include broken windows of your car a week later or abusive graffiti on your house wall to embarrass you. That makes us unpredictable.

Imagine a young man is going to propose to his girlfriend for the first time. Even if he has known her for a long time and claims to understand her well, he is unsure of how she is going to react to that. She can accept his proposal or say—'I like you; can we just be friends?' The possibilities are immense, and she should choose one. This unpredictability in any interpersonal relationship is what makes it the most difficult problem to solve. It is more difficult than complex mathematics because there are two random (well, almost) variables interacting with each other.

With the gift of choices, we get the bane of responsibilities. We are supposed to be accountable for the choices we make. If our choices are wrong, we can be tried in the court of law. The criminal justice system is based on the hypothesis that the murderer always had a choice of not committing the crime. Since the person knew the consequence of the act and still committed the crime, he must be punished for the same. He can't argue that he could not exercise his free will. If somehow it can be proven that the person did not have the mental abilities to understand the consequences of his actions, the punishment can be reduced or pardoned, as in the case of juveniles or mentally disabled ones.

Free will has been one of the founding hypotheses of psychology. It presumes that humans are rational beings who always make appropriate choices for themselves. The behavioural science is primarily the study of these choices made by people. These choices influence their learnings, and they improve it over time. There is a famous quote saying, 'What we are today, is due to the choices we have made in the past'. This is also an empowering thought—we can be what we want to be if we make the right choices.

Do We Really have Free Will?

Recent discoveries in neuroscience have dented this understanding of 'free will'. Some of the neuroscientists have postulated that almost everything that we do is controlled by the subconscious or non-conscious brain. The subconscious brain is not controlled by our free will. At some stage of the decision-making process, the conscious brain is informed of the decision made by the subconscious brain. That is when we become aware of it. However, by this time the action is already initiated. By this logic, the neuroscientists are reinforcing the theory that humans are no different from an animal. This essentially means that we have no free will. This is a very unsettling theory for the psychologists—this strips human of the exceptionalism of rationality.

Brain Experiments on Free Will

There was a famous experiment done by neurologist Benjamin Libet in the 1980s on neural aspects of free will. He told the subjects to watch a special clock and record the time at which they wanted to move their wrist. He asked the subjects to note the exact time when they felt the urge to do so. They were asked to act fully as per their free will. The EEG scanners were already connected to their brain to measure the brain activities.

The EEG revealed that an electrical potential occurred several hundred milliseconds before people reported a conscious decision to move their wrist. This was called readiness potential. This indicated that the brain had already decided to move the wrist much before the conscious self was made aware of it. The conscious awareness had no agency over the brain's action. This brought up the concept of 'neuro-determinism'.

There was another experiment on similar lines with more dramatic outcomes. The experimenter placed his subjects facing a screen on which photographic slides were projected. The subjects were asked to press a button to move the slide projected in front of them. They were perfectly at their free will to choose when they wanted to press the button. The subjects were also wired (EEG signals) to detect the readiness potential in the area of the brain that is believed to control the hand movements. The EEG signals captured the peak electric waves in the brain at the time of decision making.

There was a small trick in the experiment that the subjects were not aware of. The slide movement was directly connected to the EEG signal instead of the button in the hand. There was no connection of the hand-pressed button with the slide projector. Whenever the EEG detected the readiness potential, the slide automatically moved. The subjects were shocked to see that that the slides moved even before they pressed the button. Somehow the slides pre-empted the subject's free will. They still believed that they were moving the slides by pressing the button while there was no connection.

The analysis of the results proved that slides moved much before the subjects became aware of their decision and pressed the button. This meant that the subjects become aware of their intent (in this experiment, pressing of a button) much after (200 milliseconds) the EEG signals from the brain denoted that the brain had decided to invoke its motor action. So, the sequence was—first, the brain decided that it had to act, started acting and much later informed the conscious self. At this point, the subject became aware of the decisions, by then the decision was already executed by the brain. The subjects were no actors but acted upon by their brain activities. This essentially alluded that humans have no free will and all they do is an outcome of their brain activities; they are just spectators. If we study the brain activities, we can possibly predict the action that humans are going to take.

In fact, the neuroscientists went a step further to explain that brain creates this illusion that we have free will. To do that, it rewrites the memory in the sequence that 'will' came first followed by the motor actions. The brain tricks us to believe that we are in control while we may just be a playground for our neural activities. To demonstrate this, a study was undertaken by Adam Bear and Paul Bloom of Yale University. The subjects were shown five white circles and were asked to select which one of them would turn red, in a rapid sequence. They could note if their prediction was right, wrong or they did not have time to select. Statistically only 20 per cent of the times the subjects could have been correct, but the subjects reported much higher correct choices. The scientists concluded that the minds of the subjects were swapping the order of events for the subjects to believe that it was they who were controlling the events. It is a nice and happy feeling to have, and the brain might have evolved to reward this perception. It is harmless until it goes too far, like we believe that we are controlling the weather.

Most real-life decisions are much more complex than the pressing of a button to move the slides, so we are still far off from being able to predict human behaviour from brain waves. However, these experiments are very unsettling to psychologists and philosophers because it hits the very basis of philosophy that there is nothing called 'free will'. Take away free will and there will be nothing like behavioural psychology or philosophy. This also disrupts our social and moral understanding when we can argue that we have no control over our actions. It takes away our human exceptionalism over animals.

These experiments on free will have been at the centre of controversy between neuroscientists and psychologists. Predictably, more people still favour the psychologists' version of free will because it is reassuring that we are rational human beings. The judges in the criminal courts are never going to accept neuroscientists' arguments even though the scientific experiments may prove so.

Free Will and Paradox of Choices

We believe more choices are better. We like to visit shops offering many varieties of products. Psychologists Sheena Iyengar and Mark Lepper conducted a study with jam in an upscale food market. On day one, they put on the display table, 24 varieties of the gourmet jam. The second day, they displayed only 6 varieties. Both days, the shoppers could taste and buy the jam as they chose. The findings of the experiment were remarkable. While more people visited the shop the first day, they were only one-tenth likely to purchase, compared to the second day. This experiment suggested that more is less when it comes to the decision to purchase. Not only this, but people with lesser options were also more likely to be satisfied with their decision compared to the other group.

On a philosophical level, free will gives us power to construct our realities in a way we would like. We can believe in the science and laws of physics, or God and unexplained superpowers. Progressively, we have chosen more to believe in science. We have earned our freedom from dogmas and unsubstantiated teachings. We are unburdened from past values and beliefs of the society. We can question everything and reject it if we are not convinced of the rationality. We are completely free. This freedom however is a double-edged sword because it brings back the question of making choices and finding meaning and purpose of our existence. The noted existentialist philosopher Jean-Paul Sartre explains this anguish of freedom:

> "Man is condemned to be free; because once thrown into the world he is responsible for everything he does."

Key Takeaway Points:

1. Animals are automata. They have very limited choices to make, and their reactions are highly predictable. Confronted with a situation, they chose either fight or flight.

2. We, as humans can select our actions from numerous possibilities. We are presumed to possess free will and ability to select the correct choice. This makes us unpredictable but interesting at the same time.

3. We are also presumed to have the ability to predict the outcome of our actions based on our ability to imagine various scenarios. We are supposed to be aware of the consequences of our actions.

4. The fundamental underlying assumption in philosophy and psychology is that humans have free will. This is the basis of behavioural studies and moral values.

5. The existence of free will is also very empowering because it establishes that we can be what we want to be. If we make the right choices, we can achieve any level of success.

6. The guiding principle of the criminal justice system is the existence of free will amongst

us. Every person can exercise his or her free will to not commit a crime and be aware of the consequences in case he does.

7. The existence of free will is the basis of all modern institutions—a customer can choose the right product; a voter can exercise his or her voting rights, etc.

8. Neuroscientists do not agree with this definition of free will. They even question the existence of human exceptionalism on this topic.

9. Recent experiments in neuroscience indicate that the idea of free will may just be an illusion. Our activities are controlled by the neural activities in the brain and our conscious self is informed about it much later. In a way, our awareness has no agency over our actions.

10. The concept of free will continues to be a point of strong disagreement between the neuroscientists and psychologists/philosophers. The jury is still out on this.

Do Smartphones Make our Brain Smart?

Social media has taken over in America to such an extreme that to get my own kids to look back a week in their history is a miracle, let alone 100 years.

—Steven Spielberg

Vivek Wadhwa in the prologue of his book *Your Happiness Was Hacked* shares his story:

> "Sometime back I went on a cruise holiday with my wife, something that we had been planning for many years. I thought this would be a good experiment in digital absenteeism. Initially it seemed like a wonderful escape from the daily humdrum at work but soon this all changed. My mind was still preoccupied with the developments at my office.

> "I felt a strong urge to check my emails. To my agony, there was no internet on cruise. Now suddenly I was cut off from my active world. The more I tried to avoid the thought of being

disconnected, the more it came back to haunt me. My wife was happy about it, but I started feeling severe anxiety. It increased slowly and soon it spread to different parts of my body, and I started feeling pain. By the end of the third day, my condition was so bad that the moment our cruise returned, I had to be rushed to the hospital. The doctor confirmed after the check-up that I had a severe heart attack. I am sure this was triggered by the anxiety of being cut off from the network. This was when I realised that my email addiction had become so problematic."

It is not difficult to relate to the story. Most of us could have been in his place. We have all felt crippling anxiety at times. But how do we reach such a state? It does not happen suddenly.

Frog in the Boiling Water

Some of internet and social media addictions work like the boiling frog syndrome. When you put a frog in water and slowly start heating the water, the frog does not sense the danger. It even enjoys the initial warmth. The frog does not make any attempt to jump out. After some time, the water becomes too hot. Now, the frog realises the danger and tries to jump out. By that time, its muscles become too weak to jump out of the boiling pot. It eventually dies.

Some of these technological addictions today work like that. The stress keeps increasing till it overpowers us. At this stage, our brain's reward circuit is altered in such a way that we don't have control over our addictions. It works exactly like alcohol or drug addictions in people.

How Serious is the Social Media Addiction?

There was a survey in 2011, where youngsters had to choose among losing from a list of things including cosmetics, their car, their passport, their phone and their sense of smell. They could retain only two from the list. 53 per cent of those aged 16–22 years and 48 per cent of those aged 23–30 years said they would prefer to give up their sense of smell if it meant they could keep their cell phones. Today, cell phones are like our extended body parts and for many of us probably more precious than body parts.

We can very well say that every new technology had naysayers who were worried about the influence on humans. This was the same case when writing was invented. Before that, it was mostly the oral tradition of communication. People believed that writing would bring down the brain's wholesome experience to learn by watching, talking and hearing. The same fear was expressed when the telephone was invented. Some people believed that this would impair their skill of face-to-face communication. Years down the line, now we know that none of that has happened. In fact, some communication can happen more effectively in writing or on call rather than face-to-face talk.

Tech enthusiasts may argue that we eventually evolve, and our way of life improves by every new technological adoption. However, let us keep in mind that writing was invented thousands of years ago, even telephones were invented a century ago, so our brain had time to adjust to them. If there is one massive disruption that has rapidly changed the communication mechanism, then it is the advent of smartphones and internet. This may be too much for our evolutionary brain to adapt during a very short time. If there has been an information revolution in the last decade, it has been in the form of cell phones and of late, social media in the form of Facebook, Twitter, Instagram, etc. Our way of life has changed entirely but it has also affected our mind and brain.

Evolution of Social Brain

Yuval Harari in his famous book *Sapiens* talks about the evolution of human brains thousands of years ago. The reasons our brains are bigger in size compared to other animals is not because our brain must do a lot of mathematical calculations (of course we do that)—at what speed one should run if chased by a tiger. Our brains are bigger in size for an entirely trivial (well, seemingly) reason—'we love to gossip'. The excessive inquisitiveness in the lives of other fellow human beings was quite unique to homo sapiens. Since the hunter-gatherer days, 'gossip' has always consumed most of our brainpower, more than worrying for food in the jungle or protecting ourselves from animals.

Most of us would feel insulted today that we use our brain mostly for the unproductive task of gossiping and worrying about others. In psychology, it is called 'theory of mind'. The theory states that our existence and the world is intricately inter-related. This essentially means that our survival and well-being is dependent on the people and objects around us. We incessantly think about what others might think about us. This affects our own sense of well-being. If we think that others think highly of us, we feel happy about that even if there may not be any material change in our well-being. This sense of 'what others will think' is so strong that we worry about it even when we might not be there—when we are dead. Think of a man who is about to die due to some terminal disease. If he suddenly recalls that he had stored some diary notes that would show him in poor light—he would quickly move to destroy them.

It would seem that even after he is dead, he cares about what others think of him. This is a very strong emotion in each of us.

Apes don't worry so much about what other apes are thinking about them. The maximum they worry about is natural danger and other dangerous animals. Their social interactions are driven by procreational needs or individual safety. They don't need to gossip.

And thank God that humans love to gossip, because that became the basis of community living thousands of years ago. People started taking interest in other people's lives—it generated human feelings of love, hate, envy and other complex emotions. They felt happy and sad just thinking about fellow humans. Since the days of caves, humans have been social animals. The social media just captures this perennial human need that is programmed in our DNA, much the same as the evolutionary trait to reproduce.

Social media exploits the developmental bug of our 'gossip brain'. Facebook banks on the need of our mind to get constant social approvals. We look outside for the re-affirmation of our well-being. The 'likes' and 'positive comments' provide similar kicks like real-life achievements. Now there is scientific evidence that the Facebook engagements release dopamine—a neurotransmitter responsible for the sensation of pleasure, like winning a race or passing an exam.

In this age of smartphones, we are perennially connected to a network like our individual neurons are connected inside our brains. We are bombarded with numerous feeds every moment. Our brain had very little time to adjust to this internet age; we are already addicted to it.

We have become so used to staying online all the time that the thought of going offline scares us. In psychology, it is called 'fear of missing out'. Our mind gets anxious that we might miss out on some key events; we get withdrawal symptoms and sometimes panic attacks.

Inflated Self

Thanks to social media, there is little space between the things that are happening around us and the things that are happening to our self. We have expanded our sense of self. We imagine ourselves pretty much at the centre of the world and we presume everyone and everything has to work for having a positive impact on us. We believe that the world exists to keep us happy, it has an obligation to us. So we build a strong point of view for each event, every person around us. Hence an incident that in a pre-social media would have been completely irrelevant to us, has suddenly become relevant; we feel as though we are a part of it and our imaginary well-being depends on it. We constantly struggle to find our relevance in the physical world and it manifests in the overindulgence on social media.

When we browse through angry tweets, we can understand why people feel so enraged. We have lost our ability to see things without judging them. Everything has to be either good or bad. Either we like or dislike, love or hate. It divides us into binaries. The mind is always comfortable dealing with the binaries because then it knows how to react to the same with different emotions that are nothing but preconfigured algorithms of the past.

The cell phone addiction is giving rise to unprecedented problems. Children are twice as vulnerable to the radio frequency (RF) waves due to their thin skulls and bones. There was a study by American Medical Association that indicated that this excessive radiation of RF waves could possibly lead to some form of brain cancer. Only time will tell the effect of the long-term radiation on children. Many countries are waking up to the ill effects of cell phones. Some countries like the United Kingdom already have smartphone rehab centres for children as young as 13 years old. In Russia, the scientists and government officials have advised that anyone under the age of 18 years should not use cell phones. In France, marketing of cell phones for children is banned.

As per one Indian study, cell phone users who were on the phone for sixty minutes a day over four years experienced damage to the DNA in roughly 40 per cent of their cells. The main issue with the cell phones is the microwave radiation, especially within a distance of six inches; farther the device from the brain, the safer it is. One can imagine the impact of standing near a microwave oven all day; the radiation can impact various tissues and cells.

Facebook as Fake Book

Today there are 3+ billion users on Facebook, worldwide. The average person spends 2 hours a day, so in total, he or she may be spending more than 5 years of the lifetime scrolling through the Facebook pages. For teenagers, this could be as high as 9 hours per day. The problem has already reached an epidemic proportion and many people are urging to act in this regard. Some estimates post that there are 210 million people worldwide who might be suffering from internet and social media addiction.

Have you heard of a term called 'fake-a-vacation'? Today, there is a full industry that has evolved with social media.

As per a *Times* survey, as much as 30 per cent of Americans admitted to engaging in vacation doctoring, saying that they posted a photo on social media that makes it look like they were staying in a more luxurious place. For millennials, this ratio was 56 per cent.

There are many small companies that have packages for different holiday trips to places like Hawaii, Las Vegas or Disneyland that starts as low as 30 dollars. All you do is share some of your photos and the company will doctor them to make it look like you have visited the place. This can give you the online bragging rights like the ones who have visited those places.

And the sociologists say, after all it is not such a bad thing. It helps an average American avoid going in debt (1,100 dollars as per the survey) while travelling.

The popular saying has been 'Fake it till you make it'. Now it should be modified to 'Why make it when you can fake it'?

There was a much talked about story of a Dutch girl who posted about her travel to Phuket. She was seen sharing videos of eating local food, going to temples and shopping in market areas. It was a super hit and she got a lot of followers. In the end, she divulged that it was all shot in her home city in Amsterdam, many of the scenes being from her home itself after some fake staging. But she was able to fool even her friends and family members.

But why this compulsive urge to fake things? It is the way Facebook works. We pass from one highlight to another highlight of our friends' lives. When one browses through the variety of content from all kinds of people, it creates a sense of emptiness and a feeling that others' lives are more eventful. It is vanity at display. Facebook is unhappiness bundled as happiness. At Facebook, we are all alone together.

According to psychologists and family counsellors, some of these couples who post such adorable anniversary pictures on Facebook and get hundreds of likes, have very bitter relations. Slowly, Facebook is making us all fake. We are getting split personalities—one that we share on our Facebook page as having a great, happy-go-lucky life and the other one which is real, a boring self. For as much as we gloat about the selective moments of happiness that we share, we ardently wish our real life does not get revealed. All of us have a digital personality today that appears more important than the real one. We all care for our virtual image on social media. There is a new social currency that has come into existence.

Twitter as an Outrage Machine

In 2013, Jastin Sacco was on a long journey from New York to South Africa. Before she boarded, she tweeted,

> *"Going to Africa. Hope I don't get AIDS. Just kidding. I'm white!"*

> *Of course, it was a tweet in bad taste. There were many people who were offended with her tweet. But she had no idea that by the time she landed in South Africa, she would be a worldwide trend.*

> *She had only 170 followers at the time of her tweet. On knowing the enormity of the problem, the PR executive of IAC, where she worked, issued an apology:*

> *"Words cannot express how sorry I am and how necessary it is for me to apologise to the people of South Africa."*

> *However, the 11-hour gap was far too much. People were so outraged that they targeted her employer and asked them to fire her before she landed. Her employer IAC fired her eventually. Just one casual tweet destroyed her entire career in a moment.*

This story indicates many things. Of course, there are people genuinely offended by such biases and want to counter that by tweet responses. Twitter has given voice to anyone who can type. But there is also a lot of idle entertainment in that. Almost everyone takes an extreme position and expresses himself or herself fiercely. The collective outrage could even eventually destroy our right of free speech because we are all afraid of public shaming.

Twitter provides a new and direct way of arguing with strangers on any random topic. In real life, we don't start a fierce argument in public places with unknown people. We don't tend to harm people for our ideologies when we are face-to-face. We are very conscious of our image and social standing. Psychologists suggest that the proximity adds a sense of humaneness. When we don't see people on the other side, we don't exhibit those values. The aircraft bombers don't show any remorse because they don't see the impact of their actions directly. On the other hand, killing even one person from proximity evokes strong human emotions. Twitter is largely anonymous. Anonymity does strange things to human psychology; it strips us of humaneness. It also does weird things like—it makes an introvert who hardly speaks in public, a fiercely outspoken person.

Twitter has made us angry warriors; we relish in shaming people. In his book, *So You've Been Publicly Shamed*, a British journalist, Jon Ronson describes how Twitter has started the practice of public shaming that used to happen in medieval Europe. People used to assemble at the town square and publicly shame the subject in question. The practice was discontinued, not due to increasing population and decreasing number of town squares but due to greater call of compassion. Public shaming was too harsh a punishment. Twitter has restarted that at a much larger scale. Jon Ronson interviewed many people who had been subjected to such shaming and the devastation that followed in their lives. The worrying thing is that it is even more difficult to control such Twitter shaming these days.

Addiction of News

Rolf Dobelli in his book *Stop Reading the News*, starts with a confession that he has not read any newspapers in the last ten years. This has tremendously improved his quality of living. One of the reasons to avoid news he says is that because most of the news is irrelevant to us. Look at the type of news any day—Trump's tweets create an outrage, a volcano erupts in New Zealand, an Oscar-winning celebrity is caught in a scandal, a knife attack in Germany and so on and so forth. In a pre-internet era, we would have not known or bothered about any of these and still gone happily about our lives. It does not affect our immediate lives, but reading them can cause a sense of anxiety. Most news is created to spur our anxiety because evolution-wise, we are programmed to be more attentive to negative news.

If We don't Read News, How we will Acquire Knowledge?

The author argues that news does not add to your knowledge because they present the wrong aspects that sensationalise things. If a bridge breaks down while a car was moving on it, the news items focus on the person in the car. They publish the driver's personal story and tragedy in great details. However, what the news should have focused on is the bridge, how old it was, why it broke and how other such accidents could be avoided in future. This does not help the readership of the newspaper though. More breaking the news, less is the relevance of the same in our day-to-day life.

If you are interested in acquiring knowledge, read well-researched articles that present the complexity of events rather than just presenting some disconnected data points. This helps us understand things and build our own insights that we can apply in daily life. A better approach is to read weekly news magazines where events are captured with some perspective and lesser sensation.

20 years back, we needed more and more information to make better decisions, in life or business. Access to information was key to success. Today, the situation has reversed. The success

depends on how quickly one can filter the unnecessary information. Today, if you want to research any topic, first you need to weed out the unwanted things. The pattern of learning has changed from being receptive to all knowledge to filtering bulk of the unnecessary information, which essentially means focusing on right information.

So, what is the conclusion? Should we shun the social media and news?

I would say, no. Internet and social media are here to stay. We can't go back to the caves again. We can't log out from all social media and cut off from the internet. In the 21st century, we must be part of this game, but we should be aware of the ill effects and moderate our behaviour.

Social media has given power to ordinary people to reach out to any number of audiences at virtually zero cost. It has made stars out of common people like us. It serves a need to connect people. Earlier, the only way to communicate publicly was through mediums like TVs, newspapers or radios which were restricted to the powerful elite. The social media is empowering in that sense. The problem starts when we don't know how to use it in moderation. There is no user manual associated with a Facebook app. It does not even mention what is the most optimum

212 | Mysteries of Mind

way to use it. It just leaves it to the users to explore it by themselves. Imagine someone buying a car but not knowing how to drive it. The social media has become like that car today.

For all the lamenting that we do about social media, many of these technological innovations are like toothpaste. Once you have squeezed it out of the tube, you can't put it back. All that we can do is to understand the effect it has on our mind and alter our behaviour accordingly.

Key Takeaway Points:

1. Smartphones today are more like an extended organ of the body. While it has made our lives comfortable and given us free time, it has also brought in some unintended consequences.

2. We have a constant urge to stay connected all the time. It has affected our mind to such an extent that we get withdrawal symptoms or sometimes panic attacks. Psychologists call this FOMO—fear of missing out.

3. Facebook has made our lives full of vanity. We capture the highlights of our otherwise ordinary life and share it in the virtual world to get constant social endorsements. Our personalities are getting split, and we are

becoming more anxious and depressed. It is affecting our brain in an irreversible way.

4. Twitter is the medium that has made all of us angry and aggressive. In real life, we would never be as nasty to other human beings as we are behind the anonymous Twitter handles. It has caused instant distress to people, affecting their physical and mental health.

5. Most news we read daily are irrelevant to us. The newspapers add sensationalism to capture our attention. They add a bit of negativity because we are more sensitive to them.

6. We can live without reading news. It can make us happier and less anxious. If there is something relevant, people around us would tell us and we would come to know about them.

7. Social media and internet work like other addictions like alcohol. We can control the urge in the initial stage, but soon it changes our neural structure and we become dependent on them. It is no longer a choice in that case.

8. We can only be proficient in any profession (doctor, artist or author) if we free ourselves

from the distractions of the cell phone. It is important for our professional success.

9. Whatever be the side effects, but the social media is here to stay and possibly it would be impossible to shun them in future. All that we can do is manage our interactions with social media while we understand their ill effects on our behaviour and brain.

10. It is a healthy practice to go offline for a few hours in a day and have a no-screen day at least once a week.

Our Fleeting Attention

yato yet niśhcharati manaśh chañchalam asthiram
tatas tato niyamyaitad atmany eva vasham nayet
—Srimad Bhagavad Gita

(Whenever and wherever the mind wanders due to its flickering and unsteady nature, one must certainly bring it back under the control of the Self.)

Which of the qualities is more admirable—ability to focus on one task by cutting off all diversions or ability to work on multiple tasks simultaneously?

Carl Jung was one of the busiest and noted psychologists of his time. Every day, he would meet with many patients for counselling and treatment. He was well known for his understanding of this field. However, every year for a few days, he would withdraw from his busy life and go into the mountains where he literally lived in caves. This was the time that he used to reflect on his research and come up with theories that could challenge the dominant narratives in the psychology of those times, by Sigmund Freud. But this was not something that Carl Jung discovered—philosophers and scientists have been known to isolate themselves to focus on one activity at a time.

As children, we are always asked to learn to focus our attention— concentrate. It is the act of isolating our mind from all diversions and applying it to one task at hand. Most of the teaching methodology is geared to impart us that skill. One of the prime learnings for our brain during childhood days is to consciously focus on one activity. Those who are not able to focus their attention well enough are diagnosed as having what the psychologists say ADHD— attention deficit in short.

Surprisingly, when we grow up, our ability to concentrate is not the most sought-after skill. When we apply for a job in the company, the question is no longer if we can focus. 'Can you multitask?'—is the common question in a manager's job interview. They explain that we have no choice but to handle things in parallel. We are bombarded with several problems simultaneously. We believe that our success depends on dividing our attention rather than focusing on any specific one. Sometimes, we can prioritise one problem over the others, but most of the time we are forced to work with divided attention. Slowly, we forget our childhood lesson of focusing and start living with a fractured attention span.

Bane of Multi-tasking

Today even when we have choice, we prefer to do things in parallel. Thanks to the internet, cell phones and social media, we have taken multi-tasking to a completely different level. Just to give an example, when we are on our computers, we have multiple browsers open, and we switch from one application to another. We never do just one thing—sometimes reading news items, sometimes emails, looking at our social media feeds, YouTube videos and some research articles. Not only this, while doing so we might also be playing some nice music through the earphones. Then we have our cell phones always beeping once every few minutes, making sure that every notification reaches us instantly.

For our evolutionary brain, so many of these parallel stimuli could be overwhelming. The brain is not able to complete even one task before being forced to abandon that and start a new one. When we do it quite often, we lose our ability to control and direct our thoughts consciously. As a result, we have fractured attention syndrome.

Focused mind is a true luxury these days. Once during an ideation session, a colleague said, "I get the best ideas when I am in the toilet," and everyone burst into laughter. When the laughter subsided, many of us confessed that it was true with the rest of us as well. It was not only Archimedes who said *'Eureka, eureka'* while in the bathtub, but most of us have also taken many crucial decisions or chanced upon an idea while in the bathroom. There is a reason behind this—in today's time, probably that is the only few moments when we are completely alone (may not be true in the case of waterproof cell phones that people carry in their bath). Rest of the time, we fill our downtime with incessant news, text, social media feeds, etc. In fact, our brain is busier during this so-called 'idle time' than during normal work.

If today, you ask anyone how they would like to fill up their idle time—they are more likely to respond by saying some screen time rather than playing games or reading a book. They are very unlikely to say—'I am going to spend idle time in reflection, pondering or plain thinking'. But there was a time when plain thinking was considered a fun sport as well. Plato figured that thousands of years ago, when thinking for fun was in vogue—'An unexamined life is not worth living'.

A 2012 review of research studies the impact of brain's default mode (DM) on our development: When people wakefully rest in the functional MRI scanner, their minds wander, and they engage in a so-called default mode of neural processing that is relatively suppressed when attention is focused on the outside world. This default mode is essential for development of some of the active, internally focused mental processing including divergent thinking and comprehension. The psychologists call this term 'constructive internal reflection' and call for a balance between the external attention and internal reflection in the educational process.

A few years ago, we could watch a single channel on the television without getting bored. There were fewer options. Today, we switch channels continuously and hardly end up watching any programme in full. In the digital age today, we have plenty of options everywhere. Since we don't want to miss anything, it results in a reduced attention span. If a story does not interest us in the first few seconds, we change the movie. If a book does not look interesting while reading the first few pages, we stop reading that. If a speech can't hold our attention for the first few seconds, we don't sit through that. We quickly form an opinion and move on. In the electronic age that we live in today, it is important to filter out the choices, and as quickly as possible.

Why Evolution Favours Distraction?

Psychologists suggest that our brain was principally designed for distraction. It has survival benefits. Think of a time when our forefathers were roaming in the jungle. Their brains were required to constantly scan the environment to see if any dangerous animals were roaming around. The task at hand was less important than the threats from the surroundings. Today, we don't face those threats but still they are relevant in some cases. Imagine you are crossing a road engrossed in thought, and suddenly a speeding car approaches in front of you and your mind forces you to step back almost instantaneously, as a reflex action. This is possible because even if you had put your brain to peak use by giving it a cognitive challenge, it was still taking breaks and scanning for other sensory inputs. The moment it sensed any danger, it alarmed you. So, getting distracted had a life-saving advantage in this case.

Most of us have seen funny videos of people walking into a pole or falling into a swimming pool when they were too engrossed with their cell phones. Too much attention on one activity could be dangerous, especially when we are directly exposed to external environments. A healthy distraction is good in such cases.

On the other side, when we are in a non-threatening external environment like in the comfort of our home or workplace, distractions limit us from doing any cognitively challenging task. For solving a complex problem, we need the undivided attention of the brain. Since the brain has limited cognitive bandwidth, it has to shut off other energy-consuming thoughts. We need to focus—we need sustained attention. This is the principle of deep work. Any creative person needs this, be it an artist, a scientist or an author. It is not uncommon for some of these people to go into prolonged periods of 'hibernation' where they cut off all external interruptions. Deep work is a must for any significant achievement.

Deep Work and Shallow Work

Thanks to the internet and cell phone, our ability to focus and do a cognitively demanding task is becoming rare with each passing day. But deep work could be as rewarding as ever. Cal Newport in his book defines 'deep work' as a professional activity performed in a state of distraction-free concentration that pushes your cognitive ability to the limit. These efforts create new value, improve your skills and are hard to replicate. The key thing here is 'distraction free'—do we really get even a few hours every day when we can be happily offline?

The other end of the spectrum is 'shallow work'—logistical style work that we perform while often distracted. These are low-value work that can be easily replicated. Responding to scores of emails, attending meetings, and browsing through the internet and social media will fall in this category. We somehow feel the need to know everything that is happening around us but only by jumping from one headline to another. What we do is just skim through various social media posts or news items—we never read them in full. The mind just tries to catch up with this overload as much as possible but feels anxious and exhausted in the end. So, if in a job interview you are being asked about multi-tasking, you can very well conclude that it just refers to a bunch of shallow activities that does not require significant thinking.

Technically, our mind does not have the parallel processing capabilities for cognitive activities. It can solve only one problem at a time. The other processing needs to wait in a queue just like a computer process working in the round robin manner. So, here is the problem in such an architecture. There is a cost of switching from one processing to another as the changeover is not instantaneous. It leaves what is called an 'attention residue'—lingering thought for the unsolved problem. It is like this—if we spend one hour focused on a problem, probably we can solve it but if our mind is interrupted multiple times in between, the cumulative time to solve the problem will be more than one hour. In many cases, we may not be able to even solve the problem because the distracted spurts of intermittent thoughts do not add up. This can explain why shutting down all notifications on your mobile and checking emails only at a pre-designated time can increase brain productivity.

There are two types of attention—overt attention and covert attention. When we look at an object directly, we are paying overt attention. The eyes help us focus on the object. The covert attention is the ability of the brain to direct thought internally without any sensory inputs. Thanks to this ability, we can be sitting through a boring lecture in a classroom while thinking about the football match in the evening. It is this type of attention that requires extensive practice and results in more creativity.

Human attention also has a unique feature of selectively focusing on some sounds while filtering out the surrounding noises. The scientists call this 'cocktail party problem'. In a cocktail party, everyone is talking and there is a lot of noise, all mixed up. For a machine, it is difficult to find out the individual noise sources. However, if someone says your name even softly, you can hear that, and your attention turns towards the same. While doing so, your brain suppresses all the surrounding noise. This is a unique ability of the brain to suppress noise and focus on specific human voices. If you hear the audio recording of the party, you would not be able to find out when your name was said. The machines are very poor at recognising a specific human voice. With advancements in deep learning, some aspects of this problem are being understood.

In neuroscience, attention is an emerging area of study. Just like consciousness, there is no conclusive evidence, but it is expected to be an emergent property of the brain. The electrical activities in different parts of the brain compete to get under the spotlight. The spotlight comes into the conscious canvas as the attention. But soon, the signals in other parts of the brain gain dominance and push the existing thought out of reckoning. That is why thoughts are fleeting. Thoughts make our mind that keep jumping, like a monkey from one branch to another branch of the tree.

As much as attention is uncontrollable, driven by sensory inputs and our brain activities, it is also proven that our prefrontal cortex has some part of the control. That is what happens during deep thinking or complex problem-solving. This suppresses the multiple distractions that the brain faces by switching attention inward. With a good amount of practice, it is possible to eliminate our addiction to distractions, reduce our anxiety level and increase productivity and creativity in the process.

The human brain has several parts responsible for different functions of human bodies. These parts constantly interact with each other and compete for the brain processing resources. Attention is like a spotlight that keeps moving from one region in a dark jungle to another. This spotlight may move fast when we get fleeting thoughts or move slowly when we get focused thoughts. Eventually, our brain chatter can be mapped to the electrical activities of neurons that keep shifting every moment.

Imagine a waiter who moves around in a busy restaurant from one table to another. He takes the order, overhears some conversations, and then moves to another table. The attention in our brain is the virtual waiter that travels through the different brain regions. Our brain has different neuron clusters like the restaurant tables.

There are lower-order brain functions like breathing and blood circulation that happen automatically. However, there is a part of the human brain called frontal cortex right above our eyes that makes us intelligent creatures. Of all the living beings, humans have the largest size of frontal cortex and scientists believe that this is the basis of cognitive revolution that humans have gone through. This part of the brain performs an executive function that decides where the brain resources should be allocated.

Of all the living creatures, only humans can voluntarily direct their thoughts, irrespective of the sensory inputs they might be getting. This means that you can be sitting in a busy market but can voluntarily cut yourself off from all the distractions and concentrate on some other interesting thought. The power of concentration is unique to us. Power of attention is in a way power of filtration; we cut off all inputs and thoughts in the mind just to focus on one. The more we do it, the more we train our brain for higher cognitive functions.

When we get fully engrossed in a single activity and filter out all external signals, we lose the sense of time and space. When a neurosurgeon enters an operation theatre, drills a hole into the skull of the patient being fully aware that even an error of one mm can drive the person into paralysis, he is at the peak of his attention. There is no more attention left for him to attend to anything else. This is also called the 'flow' state of mind. This makes us happy. If we can achieve this level of attention even for a few hours regularly, we can solve many complex problems.

Key Takeaway Points:

1. Our mind loves distraction as it is more fun.

2. Distraction also has some survival value. In olden times when the external environment was threatening, it was necessary for the mind to continuously check for dangers.

3. As a child, the first thing we learn is the ability to focus on one activity at a time. Attention deficit severely impedes our ability to learn new things.

4. Unfortunately, when we grow up, we start multi-tasking more often. This impacts our ability for complex problem-solving.

5. Attention could be of two types—overt attention and covert attention. While overt attention deals with the direct sensory input (e.g., seeing), covert attention is our ability to think of anything irrespective of the inputs from immediate environment.

6. With the development of prefrontal cortex, humans developed the unique ability to direct their thoughts voluntarily. This gave them the ability to invent new things by concentrating their energy.

7. All great philosophers and scientists have adopted the practice of deep thinking by cutting off from the distracting work. Some of them have been known to withdraw from the external world to solemnly focus on their area of work. Deep work is always rewarding in the long term.

8. Though we can do multi-tasking, our brain only works on one cognitive challenge at a time. When we switch across multiple activities, there is loss of our cognitive abilities in the form of attention residue.

9. In today's age of internet and social media, we are unknowingly becoming a multi-tasker at every moment. This also results in our reduced attention span, increased anxiety, and reduced ability to do creative work.

10. We can consciously train our brain to pay attention to one thing by regularly engaging in a single sustained activity without disruptions. A good practice is to keep all notifications on our cell phones off.

Mindfulness

Every morning we are born again. What we do today is
what matters the most.

—Buddha

As a thought experiment, imagine you are walking in a park and you see four people sitting on a bench side by side—a toddler you, a teenager you, an adult you, and an old you with a walking stick.

Suppose you walk up to them and greet them. You ask questions and all of them respond one by one. You share your views on various topics and they share their divergent perspectives. You do see some faint commonality in their bodily features and voice, but they are too insignificant for any conclusion.

Will you recognise any one of them as you? Will you find out things common among them? Will you even notice that they have been the same person at different points in time?

Most likely, you will miss that. Unless someone tells, you will never know that it is the same you; the differences will be far more noticeable than the fewer similarities.

We are not the same person as we grow into different phases of our lives. Our thoughts, beliefs and perceptions change constantly. Our mind is in a state of churn—we are constantly evolving into a new person, mentally shaped by external or internal triggers.

The biological facts also support that. Our body is in a constant state of evolution. Every six weeks, all the existing cells of our skins are replaced by new cells. All other cells of our bodies are also renewed at periodic intervals. Even the most minute parts of our body are changing at every moment. It is said that every seven years, our body completely replaces itself. It may not be visually evident, but biologically we are a new self continually—constantly evolving.

If our mind is changing constantly, our body is evolving at every moment—we are nothing but turbulence personified. But isn't this unsettling? For our identity, we need some stability. We need some anchor to explain the concept of self—something that does not change.

That is why the concept of soul is so appealing. Most religions talk of soul as the eternal anchor that is constant over our lifetime, even after death. A famous verse in Bhagavad Gita defines *atman* (soul) as formless, shapeless and limitless. It does not possess any physical properties. The soul is birth-less, eternal, imperishable and timeless and is never destroyed when the body is destroyed.

> *nainaṃ chindanti śastrāṇi nainaṃ dahati pāvakaḥ*
> *na cainaṃ kledayantyāpo na śoṣayati mārutaḥ*

(No weapon can cut the soul into pieces,

Nor can it be burned by fire,

Nor moistened by water,

Nor withered by the wind.)

Most religions consider existence of soul as the central pillar of human belief. Without soul, there would be no religion, as it will lose its mass appeal. Even philosophers clung to the idea of soul during early days. As for empirical science, it can't ever prove a negative statement. It is like proving that unicorns don't exist on Earth. It is true that no one has ever seen a unicorn, but it can also be possibly true that someone, someday, might see a unicorn somewhere. So, it is impossible to prove that there are no unicorns on Earth. The same can be said about the existence of soul.

One of the fiercest oppositions of the Darwinian evolution theory emanates from the religious thinkers for this reason. Churches considered this as the biggest threat to their existence. Darwin's evolutionary theory denies the existence of anything which is constant, not even soul. It postulates that variation in each species is key to their survival. Positive variation gets passed on as part of natural selection while the unfavourable variation dies out. All the species essentially are in a state of constant churn biologically.

How do we Measure Change?

Change is always measured with respect to time. If there was no time, there would be no perceivable change. Incidentally, only humans have a concept of time. It is the most important invention of our cognitive brain. As humans, we have a past, present and future. Our life revolves around time. Our mind conveniently toggles amongst the past, present, and future.

Animals on the other hand, know only the present; they don't ponder about the past or can't conceive of any future. There is no way you can convince a hungry monkey to preserve a banana for the next day if it finds one. If a hungry ape sees some fruits, it will eat them without worrying about food for the next day. It does not know of tomorrow or draws lesson from the past. Try explaining the concept of tomorrow to your dog and you would know that they have nothing called deferred gratification. For them, everything is momentary and instantaneous; the present trumps the future.

Humans behave entirely differently. You can easily convince a man to stay hungry if he expects some better rewards in the future, even something as imaginary as the afterlife. In fact, we are more interested in our future rather than the present. That is why deferred gratification (where you postpone your present reward for a more prosperous future) is considered such a virtue for us. There is a famous 'marshmallow experiment' conducted by Stanford University in the 1960s.

Kids at the age of four years were given a marshmallow and asked to sit in a small room, alone. The instruction given to them was very simple—they could either eat the marshmallow anytime they wanted, or they could wait till the instructor came back after a few minutes. In case they waited and did not eat the marshmallow by that time, the instructor would reward them by giving another marshmallow.

The instructor left the room after leaving a marshmallow on a table. However, a camera captured the activities of the kids during this time. Of course, they were tempted to eat while the instructor was away, but some of them resisted that till the waiting time. Some kids could not wait, and they ate up the marshmallow quickly.

But the experiment did not end here. These kids were studied for several years into teens and adulthood. The experiment revealed that those who waited and resisted the temptation had better SAT scores, were better planners, more successful in life and less prone to overeating than the impulsive kids.

This experiment proved the value of deferred gratification for general success in life. Humans are investment-centric and that is the basis of our economy and our civilisation as well. We all believe that our future is going to be better than our present. We may be happier, wealthier, stronger, etc. We all look forward to our future. It may have some survival benefits as well. With all our cognitive power, we can imagine a future but if we believe that our future is going to be worse, we are going to be miserable and unhappy. We will never look forward to life. We can get depressed and eventually lose interest in living.

Is Time a Human Invented Illusion?

Time is possibly the most important concept using which we make sense of the world around us. If there were no time, birth and death would be the same event; they are just separated by the dimension of time. Interpretation of time must have brought the cognitive revolution in humans. Without the concept of time, the cave dwellers may have been as good as animals.

Time is represented in our brain as memory. We identify ourselves as a series of traits that are nothing but highlights of those memories. Our present identity is always derived from our past and leads us into our future. Memory is the scientific counterpart of soul that provides an anchor to the self. If you were to lose your memory one day, you may as well lose your personality and be a completely new person.

On a contrary note, this division of time into past, present and future could well be a figment of imagination for the human mind. As Einstein's relativity theory says, time is not absolute and even the concept of past and present could well be an illusion. If you move at a higher speed, time slows.

In a famous thought experiment, one of a pair of twins, stays on Earth while the other twin leaves Earth in a spaceship that moves at the speed of light or more. When after several years the spaceship returns to Earth, the twin on Earth has grown old while the one who went in the spaceship has just gotten into the teens. Time flows faster for the twin on Earth while it is much slower for the spaceship twin who is moving at a very high speed. This signifies that one can defy aging if one can move fast enough. Time can slow down for him.

It seems very weird, but there is empirical evidence of this theory as is measured by atomic clocks in high-speed spaceships. According to this theory, the present, past and future are not separable; it depends on the speed of the observer.

Even the concept of 'now and here' is not absolute. Imagine someone in a far-off star that is thousands of light years away, observing things on Earth. They might see that Earth still has dinosaurs. Their concept of the past, present and future could be entirely different from those of people on Earth. Similarly, when we see the stars at night, we might be seeing a snapshot that existed several thousand years ago. What is 'now' for us on Earth is 'past' for those stars. So, the concept of past, present and future gets mixed up based on who is the observer and who is being observed. They are not absolute.

What does this fusion of past, present and future mean for the human mind? Well, first it is very difficult to comprehend, but if we could ever assimilate them, we could get rid of our worst companion—worry. If there was no past and there was no fear of the future, we could all live happily in the present moment.

During the hunter-gatherer days and before the cognitive revolution, possibly our forefathers lived without the concept of time. They moved from one place to another, hunted when they felt hungry and did not worry about the next day or what happened years ago. The future was so unpredictable that there was no point of any planning. They were at the mercy of Mother Nature; there was very little that they could control. Their lives were simple—from one moment to another.

Then the agricultural revolution happened. With agriculture came the planning for the future crops and the need to know the past cycle of weather, rain, etc. Humans were not content with satisfying their immediate hunger, but they wanted to make sure that they had enough food for the coming weeks, months and years. They not only had to produce the grains but construct large granaries to store them. With storage came the risk of theft. Suddenly, the future was scarier than the present—worries started dominating our momentary existence. The modern mind of today has evolved from the agriculturist brain. Worry is the result of vagaries of our mind. Time acts as a fundamental catalyst in this subversion.

So, what is the takeaway? How do we stop our mind from drifting?

One simple solution could be to refocus our mind into our body. Our body is more in harmony with nature, it lives in the present. If the mind stays within the realm of our body, we may live a far happier life. While the life force during hunter-gatherer days was driven by our physical bodies, after cognitive revolution it was the brain that was calling the shots.

One emerging area of exploration in this field is called 'mindfulness'—ability of our mind to stay in the present and live in the moment rather than worrying about the unseen events of the future or events of the past. This essentially means that we need to slow down in this age of fast-paced life, physically and more so mentally.

The mind does not care about the absolute speed of events or activities. It only senses the relative speed, relative to the previous activity it was engaged in or what it perceives externally. Just like we feel as though we are not moving in a flight at a 1000 km per hour, our mind recognises the activity of the things only in our proximity. The more active we become, the more our mind craves for further activity to get a similar kick. The mind only knows the acceleration, not the uniform speed. That is why today, people with more active lives could be more prone to boredom and depression.

The best way to kill boredom is to really do something very boring and do it till the time the mind starts perceiving it positively. The most boring thing for the mind is 'to do nothing'. Another name of doing nothing is 'meditation'. When you force the maddening craving for activity to come to a screeching halt, the mind's zero error is reset, and it can start perceiving the happiness in the small events around us.

Why do we Need to Slow Down our Mind?

We are too preoccupied by our mind. Bringing the mind to a halt brings us more in consonance with the body. When our body and mind are in sync, we are most likely to experience happiness and contentment. In our daily lifestyle, most of the times our physical body is stationary but the mind is racing at high speed. We need to increase physical activity of the body and reduce the speed of thoughts in our mind.

A racing mind is nothing but a source of worries. Our mind has evolved to consider the worst outcome as the most probable outcome even if in reality, it could be far less likely. We assign undue weightage to the unfavourable outcome and prepare ourselves for the worst eventuality. Again, this is an evolutionary process and it was very much required when our ancestors faced a lot of external dangers. For example, even if there was the faintest probability that an animal hiding in the bush could be a lion, our mind pressed the panic button and we started running at top speed. More often, it could well be an illusion, just like we think that a small rope is a snake in the dark. The primary objective of our brain has been to keep us safe. In doing that, it played extra safe to the extent of being irrational and foolish at times.

During pre-historic days, this was fine from the survival point of view since there were many external threats. In the lymbic system of our brains, there is an interesting organ called 'amygdala' that orchestrates such a fight or flight response and channelises the entire body resources to counter the perceived threat. Today, the dangers in our daily lives have reduced but our pre-historic brain has still not adjusted. We need not have that fatalist view and assign excessive weightage to the worst outcome. That way, we can keep a sense of realism intact.

What mindfulness does is that it creates a space between our mind and the external world and events. It creates a pause between our stimuli and our reactions. It allows us to appreciate that most things around us just happen; they don't have to happen to us. Many things exist, they don't exist exclusively for us. Our peace of mind will be driven not by how much the world events are beneficial to us, but how much we can train our mind to slow down.

Key Takeaway Points:

1. We are constantly changing, physically and mentally. Our body cells are replaced every six weeks; our thoughts and believes undergo a drastic change over time.

2. The thought of this massive change is unsettling for us. We desparately try to find an anchor in this maddening change within us.

3. The concept of the soul being timeless, formless and limitless is our attempt to find constancy in the rapid change within us and externally in the environment. The soul is central to most religions.

4. Darwin's evolutionary theory tells us otherwise. The law of natural selection states that evolution is based on mutations, events that could be biologocal or environmental.

5. Our hunter-gatherer forefathers always lived in the present. The environment was too unpredictable to worry about the future. We had almost no control on nature.

6. With the advent of agricultural revolution, we developed some control of nature. We could plan for things in advance—seeds, planting crops, etc. We started understanding the

change and also predicting them to some extent.

7. Change is always a function of time. Time could very well be a cognitive invention of humans. Humans can imagine a future and think about the past. Animals don't have any concept of past or future.

8. The ability of deferred gratification make humans a better planner and more successful in life. However as humans, we take it too far in our daily lives. Our mind has a tendency to race past the present and worry about the future.

9. One of the most helpful habits we could inculcate today would be to train our mind to stay in the present, just like our body that is in harmony with nature. Mindfulness is a technique to control the fight or flight response of our mind.

10. Though it may sound ironical, one of the ways to avoid boredom is do boring activity till the brain finds it enjoyable. It is the good old way of relaxing by doing nothing.

Reality or Illusion?

Reality is merely an illusion, albeit a very persistent one.

—Albert Einstein

Imagine if the world had no colour and was soundless; if the food did not have any taste or the flowers had no smell; if we could not sense an object being cold or warm, soft or hard. In summary—what would it have meant living in a world without our senses. The world would have been pretty much bland, and who would care to live in such a boring world?

In computer language, the above senses will be called inputs. Our sensory organs act like inputs to our brain that has to make sense of everything happening around us. Let us call that 'objective reality'—as things are. These objective inputs need to be first encoded in electric neural signals and then decoded to interpret what they mean. Each sense sends its input to the brain that has to create a model of the external world by combining them. There are three steps involved in converting the external inputs as meaningful interpretations—encoding, decoding and synthesising. All three of them are complex processes and prone to error. Hence, the brain model of the world could be different from the way they are.

Brain as a Story Teller

Let us take an example of processing of one of the sensory inputs—colour. In objective reality, there may not be anything like colour. The wide range of electromagnetic waves are reflected from an object; only a limited range in that is captured by the photoelectric cells in our eyes. We call it visible range. When these photons hit our retina, they are converted into electric signals and sent to the visual cortex at the back of our brain called V1 region. It then projects the signal on other segments called V2 and V4. V4 segment assigns certain wavelengths as colour and we see our world as colourful. So, it is not the specific wavelengths but our brain's interpretations that makes us see these colours.

Why do we identify these specific radiations as colours? There are so many other radiations like radio waves, alpha waves, gamma waves, etc., that our eyes can't detect, and for us they don't exist. The claim is that those radiations were probably not important for our evolution, so our brain did not adapt to them. A red, green and blue was probably more important to identify food so our brain evolved to see them. If an apple emitted gamma waves, we might have developed the ability to see the gamma waves. The point here is that our brain alters the objective reality to suit our subjective well-being. What we see as colour is not how different radiations are, but how they are helpful to us for survival and evolution.

An objective reality is like a camera that just captures the things as they happen. It does not add any interpretation—it does not tell any story. The human eye in a way is like that camera that just captures the pictures transmitted to the brain. The sight of a running dog in the street changes every millisecond. A high-resolution camera will capture that as thousand different pictures at different moments. Our eyes also capture these pictures and send these signals to our brain.

The brain is where the magic happens. The brain deconstructs the images in its own neural language. Some parts of our brain capture the edges and orientations, some capture motion of the objects, whereas some tap into the memory segment and together they all combine to tell ourselves that a dog is running in the street. This is where the brain accords a meaning to the external event or the objective reality. In doing so, the brain does not strictly go by what the eyes see; in fact, our eyes move and flicker while taking pictures and if one were to feed this into a video camera as we see, it would be jerky frames almost awful to watch or comprehend. The brain alters the reality in a way that we can make sense of our environment and take actions to protect ourselves. In telling a story, our brain extrapolates.

The brain also combines the inputs of different senses to make meaning out of them. If our eyes send some image of an animal moving towards us and our ears send a roaring noise—our brain has to interpret that as life-threatening and prepare us for running away. This processing of different sensory inputs by decoding and synthesising them is the 'subjective reality' for us. This processing can be different for different humans, and hence the same reality can be interpreted differently.

Every moment, our brain is telling us a story of what is happening in the outside world. Our brain has no eyes or ears. It is housed in a tightly packed cranium that cannot perceive light, sense or odour. All it can sense is a series of electrical signals connected through billions of neurons. Using these signals, it invents a story of the outside world every waking moment. This story is the best-case projection based on the sensory inputs and our brain processing. Our reality is the fictional story that the brain creates for us.

We see that more clearly when one or more of these processes go wrong—our reality changes. One of the well-known problems in colour processing is called synesthesia. The patients of this problem always see a colour when they see a number—for example, 5 is always red, 3 is always blue. Renowned neurosurgeon V S Ramachandran in his book *The Tell-Tale Brain* explains this phenomenon as follows:

> "Whenever Francesca closes her eyes and touches a texture, she experiences a vivid emotion: denim, extreme sadness; silk, peace and calm; orange peel, shock; wax, embarrassment. She sometimes feels subtle nuances of emotions. Grade 60 sandpaper produces guilt, and grade 120 evokes 'the feeling of telling a white lie'.

> "Mirabelle, on the other hand, experiences colours every time she sees numbers, even though they are typed in black ink. When recalling a phone number, she conjures up a spectrum of the colours corresponding to the numbers in her mind's eye and proceeds to read off the numbers one by one, deducing them from the colours. This makes it easy to memorise phone numbers.

"When Esmeralda hears a C-sharp played on the piano, she sees blue. Other notes evoke other distinct colours—so much so that different piano keys are colour coded for her, making it easier to remember and play musical scales.

"These people are not crazy, nor are they suffering from a neurological disorder. They and millions of otherwise normal people have synesthesia, a surreal blending of sensation, perception and emotion. Synesthetes (as such people are called) experience the ordinary world in extraordinary ways, seeming to inhabit a strange no-man's-land between reality and fantasy. They taste colours, see sounds, hear shapes, or touch emotions in myriad combinations."

In above cases, the reality is perceived differently because the wiring in our brain may be different. The subjective reality is created by our brain by the sensory inputs and its own processing. They could be vastly different for different people. We all live in two different worlds—one that is objective and one that is subjective. The objective world is what things are, and subjective world is the story that our brain tells us. Our brain is creative—it twists reality and sometimes invents it. That is why we all experience the same world so differently.

Why do we Bother About the Subjective and Objective Reality?

Our well-being and happiness do not depend on the objective world to a large extent. It is the subjective reality in our mind that matters. We all wonder how a rich celebrity who has everything in this world suddenly falls prey to bouts of depression and in some rare cases, even commits suicide. Their subjective experience of their own lives could be entirely different from what we would see through our own lenses.

Psychologists attempt to study this by measuring the observable behaviour. They say feelings can't be measured, so there can't be any empirical science based on that. But stimuli and behaviour can be measured. So, they discount the thoughts and feelings and focus on explaining a situation by the external behaviour of the person. They take behaviour as the proxy for our subjective experience or feeling. This is also called behaviourism—a separate focus area in psychology. But we all know that feeling something and demonstrating similar behaviour could be two different things. I may feel very angry in my mind but sit in my chair completely calm. How can anyone measure the anger in my mind without me telling how angry I feel? The only way we can measure anger accurately is when the person himself talks about it.

Another problem with behaviourism is that measurement can change the behaviour itself. It is something like an alien coming into our room and asking us to perform certain activities while they observe our behaviour. Despite our best efforts, we may not be able to display completely natural behaviour. This may well relate to Heisenberg's uncertainty principle in atomic theory which states that our attempt to measure the properties of a sub-atomic particle may change it. So, we can never measure it beyond a precision. Subjective reality and behaviourism can relate to this theory well.

And what if we ourselves are not able to articulate our feelings correctly? Can the psychologists identify that?

There was an interesting experiment done by psychologist David Rosenhan in 1973 at Stanford. He identified seven healthy patients (included himself as the eighth) as pseudo-patients and gave them a feigned psychiatric illness by saying that they heard voices in their brain. They answered all other questions perfectly normally except for this 'hearing voices' disorder. They gained admission to psychiatric hospitals. After they were admitted, the patients said they no longer heard the voices, and they were fine now. The experiment was to identify how long it would take for the hospital staff to recognise that they were completely normal.

It seems the average time taken was 19 days.

The above experiment called into question all psychoanalytic techniques that failed to detect the perfectly normal pseudo-patients who were misreported.

Offended by the above experiment, the hospital administration challenged Rosenhan to send the disguised pseudo-patients once again whom their staff would identify. This time, they identified 41 patients out of 193 with psychiatric disorders. The catch—Rosenhan had sent no pseudo-patients this time, they were all real patients. This experiment sent a shockwave throughout the mental health professions. Rosenhan wrote a paper – 'If sanity and insanity exist, how shall we know them?'

Haven't we heard this dialogue very commonly in our movies, 'You don't understand my feelings!' The whole movie is about discovering the same. The fact is that our subjective experience is uniquely personal; others can only guess based on demonstration of some external behaviour, but no one can really know others' exact feelings. This leaves the field of philosophy open to the inquiry of subjective experience of the world.

What does neuroscience say about our subjective experience? Well, they say that science still can't study that because it is not a measurable property.

How can we measure how angry or sad you feel? We can try fMRI or EEG to record blood flow or electric signals in parts of the brain but that is a very vague representation, and we are far from accurately measuring it. The problem with components of subjective experience like emotions and consciousness is that they are network properties that kick in only when billions of neurons interact in a unique way, still a non-simulatable problem for our computers.

The subjective experience very well emerges from the wiring of our brain, this we know. What we don't know is how. This becomes evident in a very weird phenomenon called phantom limb.

The patients of phantom limb were the people who had their hand or leg amputated. Most of these patients were soldiers during the war who suffered injury. Quite a few of them reported a very strange phenomenon after amputation—they said they felt pain in their hand and leg even though they knew that the limb no longer existed. The patients even felt embarrassed to tell this to the doctor, thinking they were crazy. This illness was known as phantom limb.

When neurosurgeons studied the patients further, they discovered the underlying reason. Our brain has a somatosensory cortex that has got a map of the entire body. Each one of our body parts where we feel any sensation is represented there in a different proportion. In case of these patients, though the limbs were amputated the corresponding neural circuit was still active. For the brain, the limb still existed. Though this patch did not get any physical sensory input, it got activated sometimes due to neighbouring neurons or some random input. This caused itching or pain sensation in the amputated limb.

When the doctors explored further, they discovered that this was triggered by touching some other body part like say, the cheek. The explanation provided was that in absence of any sensory input, the nearby patches of neurons extend themselves in the amputated limb's neural area, causing this strange phenomenon.

V S Ramachandran talks about this illness in his book, Tell-tale brain. *He suggests an out-of-the-box solution—called mirror therapy. This suggests the patients with one amputated hand (the phantom limb that was causing pain) to place the normal hand opposite to a sidewise mirror and mimic the movement through the mirror image as if the original hand existed. The brain gets the fake visual input that it can move the amputated hand. This relieved the patient of the pain.*

In this example, the experience of the person is not driven by the reality but the illusive map in his brain. Essentially what Ramachandran does in the therapy, is to fool the brain to believe that it is able to move the amputated hand.

The world is colourless and dark. It is our brain that lights it up and makes it interesting. Modern philosophers explain this as 'brain in vat' conundrum. They ask us to imagine our brain is housed in a small jar and is being fed all electric signals through our neurons (just as in the real brain). We are seeing the physical world and sensing things. But factually, nothing is happening. It's just that our brain is being fed those signals. Now can you prove that you are not the 'brain in the vat'? Well, you can't prove it. We may all be just 'brains in the vat'. This conundrum captures the dilemma of objective vs subjective reality.

In the quantum theory, the understanding of reality gets a completely new perspective. As per the Schrodinger's cat example, the cat in the closed box may be dead or alive at the same time. In traditional science, either things may exist or not exist, and we can measure the same, but in quantum theory there is a third state possible where it can exist or not exist simultaneously. It is only when we try to measure the same that it comes out as one unique state. It means that the reality is enforced by our consciousness and only when we try to measure the same. Einstein never liked this idea that nature is so uncertain. He believed that we live in an orderly world and everything happen for a reason. Peeved by the quantum uncertainty, he once commented, "Does the moon cease to exist if you don't look at it?" It is same as saying, "Does the falling tree still make a sound if no one is watching?" or to take it to an extreme, "Do you not exist if I don't look at you?" As a child, I had a strong suspicion that the hands of the clock wouldn't move if I didn't check it. Here, physics and philosophy get mixed up. Reality in that way is purely an anthropomorphic view and we can never know the absolute reality without actually affecting it in an attempt to know.

The ancient philosophers in India had probably some idea of this complex processing inside our mind and how error-prone it can be. That is why they called the world that we see *maya* (magic or trickery). It asks us never to fall for the things that our senses tell us, because they may not be true at all. We must have a sense of scepticism about every story that the brain tells us. The sky appears blue, but it is just the reflection of light through space. The Vedanta philosophy describes this as an interplay of *brahman* (objective consciousness) and *prakriti* (nature). *Brahman* is the unchanging constant that perceives the changing *prakriti*, creating this perception of our physical world called *maya*. It does not say that the world does not exist but insists that it may not be a true reflection of reality. Don't take it at face value.

So, what is the solution even if we know that the world is *maya?* The sixth century philosopher, Shankara captures this in '*brahma satyam jagan mithya, jeevo brahmaiva na parah*' (*Brahman* is true reality while the world is false; there is no difference between *brahman* and the self). Just like a coiled rope looks like a snake at night and closer examination reveals it is just a rope, it is the reflection and meditation that gives us a more balanced sense of *brahman*. The *maya* is the veil of ignorance that must be cleared though training of mind via Yoga.

Key Takeaway Points:

1. We live in two worlds—the objective reality as things are, and subjective reality as we perceive them as experience and feeling.

2. The process of perceiving is multi-step and complex. It involves encoding the sensory inputs as electrical neural signals and decoding them. The brain also synthesises the inputs of different sensory inputs to create a coherent story.

3. Subjective reality that we experience is a twisted reality—a story that our brains tell us based on our own memory and internal brain wiring. Sometimes our brain invents the reality.

4. There may not be any colour or sound in the real world, it is our brain that creates it based on some external sensory inputs. We see a limited set of wavelengths as colour because our brain interprets it that way. It might have been useful for the evolutionary brain to identify a red apple.

5. The subjective experience of the same stimulus may differ from one person to another. That is why every human experience is unique and it can't be replicated.

6. The subjective reality is the most important for each of us because this is how we experience the world. Our mental states, happiness and well-being is directly driven by it.

7. There is no scientific way to measure the subjective experience of a person. The only way to know is when the person explains himself. This articulation itself could be prone to error.

8. Any psychological attempt to measure our subjective experience and feelings may change the same in the process.

9. To eliminate the subjectivity, the psychologists have come up with a method to focus on the

behaviour, as it is measurable. However, observable behaviour may not be a true proxy for the subjective experience.

10. Our mental well-being is closely linked with the mental model of the world we create. We may have all the wealth in the world, but our mind can create a depressing experience of gloom and doom.

Future of Mind

You want to know how super-intelligent cyborgs might treat ordinary flesh-and-blood humans. Better start by investigating how humans treat their less intelligent animal cousins. It's not a perfect analogy, of course, but it is the best archetype we can actually observe rather than just imagine.

—Yuval Noah Harari

One of the limitations of our mind has been that it can only exist in our body, more precisely within our brain. For all our human existence, the mind has been trapped in our bodies. The moment our bodies die, our minds cease to exist. Though they operate in different domains, today they are closely linked and interdependent.

Let us take a computer analogy. The body is like hardware and the mind is the software. During the initial days of computers, the software was specifically coded for the hardware. If we changed the hardware, the same software would not work anymore. Writing a computer program required intricate knowledge of the physical components of the computer. The software was trapped in the silicon chips and their interconnections. This also limited their potential use.

As a next phase of evolution, operating systems came into existence that separated the software from the hardware. The operating systems added a level of abstraction to the physical components of the computers. Now the software programmer did not bother about how the physical aspects of the computer worked. Thanks to the operating system, the same program could run on multiple hardware. The real software revolution started from that point. The same software program could take different physical forms be it a car, an aircraft, a washing machine, or a robot. The software became formless.

I think the future of mind would be somewhat similar. It will eventually break away from the body and claim its formless existence. This takes us to some of the sci-fi movies where humans may choose not to exist physically but convert themselves into upload programs. The upload program can be the substrate that can be downloaded to various physical forms like a robot, a computer or a car. The human physical form is perishable; the upload programs can easily be copied. They can live endlessly. They can choose to become immortals. Scientists say that with our medical advancements, our average age has been increasing and one day (some predict as soon as next 50 years), we may unravel ageing and overcome natural deaths. I think much before that, we might unravel our mind and break free from the bodies. We will become immortal not because of our never-ageing bodies but the substrate mind.

The Human Connectome Project aims to document every pathway in the brain at the neuron level. This is like documenting 100 billion neurons with each connection up to 10,000 other neurons. Though it is a gargantuan task and far from completion, it may well create a blueprint of the human mind that can be decoded at the microscopic level. If we can do the same (and there is a big if), we might as well be able to replicate this in a computer memory. Not only that, but the entire information can also be encoded in laser beams and transmitted to far-off planets. We can all become packets of energy floating in the outer space and distant galaxies. This energy can embody itself as and when it pleases. We can all become 'ghosts' and exist forever. Having said this, we must also know the limitations of the above. The information content of each neuron from a human brain may well surpass all the data on internet today. We are nowhere close to building a computer like that, currently.

To make our mind a software program that can run on any carbon or silicon body, we are yet to discover the operating system of the mind. That Holy Grail according to me is 'consciousness'. It is the most important element of our existence, but surprisingly we know the least about it.

The future of mind will be essentially driven by two factors—advancements in the field of artificial intelligence and our understanding of human consciousness. Let us take stock of the current advancements in AI, and we will come back to this topic of consciousness after that.

AI is Closing-in on Human Capabilities

We have always been curious to create machines like humans. As early as 1950, Alan Turing devised a basic test for a machine to qualify as human. It is known as Turing test and is still relevant.

> At its simplest, the test requires a machine to carry on a conversation via text with a human being. If after five minutes, the human is convinced that they're talking to another human, the machine is said to have passed the test.

Thanks to the advancement in deep learning, today we have thousands of bots that would pass this test. Google launched a Google Duplex in 2018 with a live demonstration of the automatic assistant calling a hairdresser and fixing up an appointment without the other person being aware of the same. The highlight of the demonstration was not only that the bot spoke fluent colloquial English with a local accent, but the bot added the pauses like a normal person would do. Obviously, we have gone much beyond the Turing test today.

For a long time, chess was supposed to be the exclusive citadel of humans and a symbol of their cognitive proficiency. In 1997, IBM's Deep Blue defeated the chess grandmaster, Gary Kasparov. Since then, computers have far outclassed humans in chess so much so that the judges look out for the chess players who try to cheat by using computers. These programs do not need external training; they can play with themselves and within hours, can attain the proficiency that humans have acquired over several decades. They can be more creative and original than humans.

Let us talk about memory. Today, supercomputers can store more information than an average human brain with 100 billion neurons. The same is true for computing power, which has long been exceeded by AI machines with petaflops. For some time, we believed that computers could never learn, and they needed to be hard wired for certain goals. With neural networks and machine learning, that citadel is increasingly getting invaded. Today, AI can recognise images and voices with better accuracy than humans and we are still at the early stage of AI development. All three basic components of human intelligence—memory, computations and learnability have been successfully exceeded by AI.

When Lee Sedol, the best player of Go, a game played for thousands of years by millions, was defeated by Google's AlphaGo, the most common quote on Chinese social media was:

"You lost and you cried, the computer won but it did not smile."

The purpose of presenting the above argument was that today, AI has comprehensively beaten us in what we can call human intelligence. However, they are still well short of being human. What makes us human has little to do with memory, computing and learning though they are an essential part of our intelligence. What sets humans apart from all other inanimate matter is—consciousness, awareness of self and ability to relate to the world around us. We can experience things, tell stories about them, and feel happy or sad. A robot or an AI can't experience that. A self-driving car can go around the city, and capture all the images but still can't experience any feelings. When we die—it is our consciousness that is extinguished even though the physical form can stay intact for some time.

So, consciousness seems to be the last citadel of AI and we will have to understand it in some detail for the future of the mind.

What is Consciousness?

Max Tegmark, a physicist at MIT describes in his book *Life 3.0.*

> "Consciousness is an emergent property. It can only be observed as a new phenomenon when certain particles are arranged in specific order. He gives an example with wetness—of water, vapour and ice. He explains that it is just that the arrangement of the molecular changes that creates a new property called wetness. Similarly, it is the integrated behaviour of the particles arranged in a certain order that creates consciousness. However, we don't know what is that specific arrangement that produces consciousness and if it can be replicated."

Another school of thought says that consciousness is a subjective property and hence, can't be objectively studied in science. Apparently, it has more promise in quantum mechanics, but we are far from claiming any success.

In medical science, the study of consciousness is considered a waste of time. Doctors never talk about it much in a deeper sense. The only limited use in medicine is the level of consciousness from coma or brain death at one end, to full alertness at the other end. The medical science does not focus much on fundamental definition of consciousness and what it means in a larger sense.

Probably the most discussed occurrence of this term is in philosophy. Descartes explained it as Cartesian dualism. He described that consciousness resides within an immaterial domain (realm of thought), in contrast to the domain of material things (realm of extension). He suggested that interaction between these two domains occur inside the brain in an organ called pineal gland. This is called dualist definition. There is a contrary definition called monist definition where both consciousness and matter are different aspects of one realm of being.

And finally, there is a spiritual definition of consciousness, most often practiced as part of Yoga or meditation. Consciousness is thought to be a relationship between mind and deeper truth that is more fundamental than the physical world. From time immemorial, the monks have been quoted as rising from self-consciousness to super or cosmic consciousness as an enlightened being.

This range of definition shows how multidisciplinary complex this topic is. One needs to be a neuroscientist, a physicist, a computer engineer, a psychologist and possibly a philosopher at the same time to comprehensively study this topic. However, there is no dispute that consciousness exists, and that's what primarily makes us human.

When do we Get Consciousness?

Just as there is no common definition of consciousness, there is little agreement on when it develops in humans. There is no single snapshot in time or an event calendar that we can call out, after which we become conscious. Based on what we call the most important constituent of consciousness, psychologists have differing views on when a child becomes conscious.

For the sake of understanding, let us say there are three important constituents of consciousness (world exists, I exist, I exist because the world exists).

The world exists (**awareness**)—the infants build awareness early on, in the first few months. They start recognising others in the universe as objects and people. The sensory organs very much function though they are in the early developmental stage. Though the infant is aware of the world at this stage, it can't distinguish itself from the world. It sees the world as an extension of the self. For the child, the world and its own existence both are one.

However, slowly the child discovers that the objects and people have independent existence. They exist even when the child is not sensing (e.g., not seeing) them. This is best explained by 'object constancy principle' in child development and is the basis of development of most interpersonal relationship skills among adults. When the child sees the mother walking away from it, it starts crying because it believes that the mother ceases to exist. Only with time, the child knows that the mother has an independent existence and will come back even if she walks out at times. Similarly, the child does not go after a toy if we hide it under the blanket. For the infant, out of sight means out of existence. Most children develop this before they are 7–8 months old.

I have an independent existence (development of ego)—this is explained by mirror test (or Rouge test) where the kids are shown a mirror with rouge makeup on their face. The child with no self-awareness, point to the mirror while those with self-awareness point to their own face. By the age of 18 months, half of the children can identify their own image and point successfully to their own face rather than the mirror.

My existence and the world are intricately related (theory of mind)—this essentially means that my survival and well-being is dependent on the people and objects around us. This is essentially development of the social brain. This is the time when mind A starts thinking about what mind B is thinking about mind A. This is also the time when mind A thinks what mind B is thinking about mind C. Sometimes, mind A also thinks about itself though with limited success.

To explain whether a child has developed theory of mind, a false belief test is used as exercise—the famous Sally Anne test.

> *Sally is playing with a marble. She puts the marble in her basket before going to the bathroom. Meanwhile, Anne finds the marble and hides it in her own box. After some time, Sally returns to her room to play with the marble again. Where will she look for the marble first—the basket or the box?*

A child who has not yet developed the theory of mind will respond by saying that Sally will look for the marble in the box. The child will fail to understand that Sally has her own mind that has its own copy of truth which is different from the child. The child believes that Sally knows what the child knows. According to psychologists, we develop the theory of mind by the age of 4–5 years.

Even if most humans acquire awareness, self-awareness and sometimes rare cosmic awareness, different adults have different degrees of conscious existence. While some of us have very little awareness, others are highly conscious. Consciousness has several hierarchical layers.

We have not been able to build robots that have awareness, sense of ego or theory of mind because we don't yet understand the basic principles of these aspects. Many believe that consciousness has nothing to do with intelligence, in fact they claim consciousness is an evolutionary bug in humans. We should not worry about making the robots conscious but rather making our brain more intelligent.

Our Brain Needs an Upgrade Today

Today, human brain is trying to catch up with the technological advancements. Our brain has evolved over thousands of years to be one of the most complex data processing units. But it mostly evolved in the age when we had limited data, all that our senses could collect and remember. There was no internet, there was no Goggle or Alexa. The information deluge over the last few years may make our biological brain appear highly inadequate.

To overcome this deficiency, we may have to upgrade our brain to function adequately in this information age. Elon Musk says that soon, we may need an artificial digital plug-in on top of our brain cortex that can directly connect to the internet using high-speed wireless. Our thoughts will depend on the speed of internet downloads. Humans will not have any need to learn anything. In that case, kids will not have to go to school either. We will not require to communicate; we will just exchange thoughts like telepathy. We can download our brain to a powerful computer for processing overnight while we sleep peacefully. In the morning, we can reupload the processed data of the computer to our brain.

Today, we can record sound and pictures. In future, it may be possible to record memories and emotions. If we can record all the signals going through our hippocampus and thalamus and convert them into a software program that can be downloaded by anyone to replay, we can virtually lend our experiences to another in the most wholesome way. It will not only be the picture and sound but all our senses like smell, touch, taste as well. We may actually relive that moment and share it with others on Facebook. The Oscar winners can share their moments with others to experience the same joy and happiness. This would be like the 'brain in the vat' experiment that the philosophers mentioned earlier.

It may be possible to read remotely what one is thinking. The brain is an organ that runs on electricity. This produces electromagnetic waves that can be measured. The current challenge is that these radio waves are very weak and difficult to measure from a distance. However, using an EEG device, we can analyse these waves to make a rough prediction of what the person is thinking. Though we cannot decipher complex thoughts, there have been experiments to establish that we can find out if the person is thinking about an elephant or a car. If these instruments get more sophisticated, we may well be able to decode what a person is thinking. Just as thoughts can be read remotely, it can also be planted in another brain. Memories can be erased from someone's brain or any false memory can be planted.

We can use the same technology to operate objects remotely just by thinking about it. Today, it is being used to aid the patients who are paralysed. They can operate their prosthetic limb directly using their thoughts. In future, there is no guarantee that this may not be used to augment the ability of a healthy person e.g., why not have a stronger, prosthetic hand or leg. If we can operate it through our brain seamlessly, there is no reason that we may not trade our carbon body parts with silicon ones. In the 2014 Brazil FIFA World Cup, the opening kick was delivered by an exoskeleton that was mind-controlled by a person who was completely paralysed. We have seen how Stephen Hawking could type on a computer using mind-controlled chips.

If you read any science book today on the future of mind, it will appear like science fiction. With advancements in science, the fiction of yesteryears appears closer to reality. The boundaries are increasingly getting blurred. Most futurists see a close scientific race between the human mind and artificial intelligence, both trying to outdo each other. It is quite probable that sooner or later, both will merge.

So soon, we all may become cyborgs—when the silicon intelligence will merge with us as physical implants. We will all be connected like 'internet of brains'. It will be hard to imagine what it means to be human in that era. Thankfully, we are not yet there. Many of us would refuse to exist in that situation.

Experts say increasingly that many of the cognitive jobs can be done more efficiently by artificial intelligence. This will effectively result in humans losing even their current cognitive abilities. Most of us have weakened our ability to memorise directions and follow them. Technology is increasingly making us redundant. Yuval Harari calls this phenomenon as the 'rise of useless class'. These useless humans will automatically get downgraded to a house cat that can only play video games all day. So, while the machines are learning today, the humans are getting hooked to their cell phones and becoming dumber.

Merging of Carbon Life with Silicon Life

With discovery of digital life and superintelligence, our understanding of life itself might change. In that case we can well think of a futuristic scenario that Max Tegmark describes in his book *Life 3.0*.

"In future if someone will look at Earth from space, they will see three different zones.

"Superintelligence AI zone—this zone will have high-intelligence AI that will work on their own goal. The behaviour and actions of the machines in this zone will be so complex that human minds would not be able to comprehend. This zone will become unliveable by humans.

"Cyborg zone—in this zone the humans will exist in part human-part machine form. The humans can exist as software programs uploaded into different physical forms. This zone may be less evolved and still comprehensible by a normal human mind. This will be a silicon world in a way.

"Human zone—in this zone, super-intelligent AI and cyborg will be banned. Humans will exist only in human form, something akin to the current world with more technological advancements. This will have all other carbon lives as well."

But why will a super-intelligent AI zone and cyborg zone allow any human zone?

There could be various justifications, one of them being just as we humans allow elephants to exist even though we have technically conquered them long back. Humans can kill all the animals if they want. Instead, we have created forest zones and zoos for their protection.

Similarly, a super-intelligent AI can create a large zoo for humans. This is the promise and the fear for the future of mind.

Not everyone subscribes to the dystopian views, however. Some futurists believe that we should not fear robots. They are like our children. We all love our children, knowing well that they are going to take over us while we all fade into the background. Sometimes, we even look forward to the same with great anticipation.

Key Takeaway Points:

1. Our mind and body have needed each other for existence. They have been inseparable. Our mind is trapped in our body.

2. Mind can be thought of as a software program that runs on a very specific hardware called brain. Just as the software programs can run today on different hardware, in future, our mind can also take the form of upload programs eventually.

3. Today, artificial intelligence has already surpassed humans in various areas of intelligence be it memory, computing power or learnability. We have machines today that can beat humans easily in a game of chess. Bots today can easily pass the Turing test.

4. Despite all these advancements, there is one thing that current science has not been able to fathom—human consciousness. This is the Holy Grail of human existence, the last citadel to be conquered.

5. We know very little about human consciousness. Modern medical science considers its study as a waste of time. Psychology and philosophy have tried to understand this empirically. This topic is most studied in spirituality.

6. We have various forms of consciousness—our own existence, awareness of things around us and awareness of our relationship with the

external world. It is not clear when and how we develop this consciousness.

7. Our brain that has evolved over millions of years could still be inadequate in this information age. The machines have a clear edge over capabilities.

8. Intelligence and consciousness are two different things. While computers have beaten us in intelligence, they have not yet understood the building blocks of consciousness.

9. If we unravel human consciousness one day using AI, the carbon and silicon lives will merge. Many of us will chose to become a cyborg with different physical forms. We will also become immortal in that sense.

10. One school of thought says that just as we did not copy a bird to create an airplane, we will not need to replicate consciousness for human superintelligence. In any case future of mind will be closer to the AI machines and less like humans.

References

1. *The Tell-Tale Brain* by V S Ramachandran

2. *The Science of Mind Management* by Swami Mukundananda

3. *Bhagavad Gita for Millennials* by Bibek Debroy

4. *The Man Who Mistook His Wife for a Hat* by Oliver Sacks

5. *Man's Search for Meaning* by Victor Frankl

6. *Until the End of Time* by Brian Greene

7. *When Breath Becomes Air* by Paul S Kalanithi

8. *Flow* by Mihaly Csikszentmihalyi

9. *Ikigai: A Japanese Secret to a Long and Happy Life* by Hector Garcia and Francesc Miralles

10. *Life 3.0* by Max Tegmark

11. *The Myth of Sisyphus* by Albert Camus

12. *The Alchemist* by Paulo Coelho

13. *Outliers* by Malcolm Gladwell

14. *Think and Grow Rich* by Napoleon Hill

15. *The Power of Your Subconscious Mind* by Joseph Murphy

16. *Inner Engineering* by Sadhguru

17. *Your Happiness Was Hacked* by Vivek Wadhwa

18. *Life's Amazing Secrets* by Gaur Gopal Das

19. *Sapiens* by Yuval Harari

20. *So You've Been Publicly Shamed* by Jon Ronson

21. *Stop Reading the News* by Rolf Dobelli

22. *Deep Work* by Cal Newport

23. *On the Shortness of Life* by Seneca

24. *The God Equation* by Michio Kaku

25. *The Monk Who Sold His Ferrari* by Robin Sharma

26. Paradox of choices—https://hbr.org/2006/06/more-isnt-always-better

27. Stanford prison experiment—https://www.prisonexp.org/

28. The reasons you procrastinate and how to stop—https://www.washingtonpost.com/news/wonk/wp/2016/04/27/why-you-cant-help-read-this-article-about-procrastination-instead-of-doing-your-job/

29. How to build a self-conscious AI machine— https://www.wired.com/story/how-to-build-a-self-conscious-ai-machine/

30. Marshmallow experiment—Stanford University - https://www.simplypsychology.org/marshmallow-test.html

31. Theory of mind— https://www.psychologytoday.com/intl/blog/socioemotional-success/201707/theory-mind-understanding-others-in-social-world

32. Sally Anne test—

    https://www.theguardian.com/science/head-quarters/2017/jan/23/sally-anne-task-psychological-experiment-post-truth-false-beliefs

33. Turing test—

    https://www.britannica.com/technology/Turing-test

34. Einstein, Bohr and the war over quantum theory—

    https://www.nature.com/articles/d41586-018-03793-2

GARUDA PRAKASHAN BOOKS

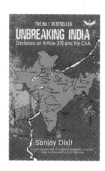

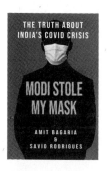

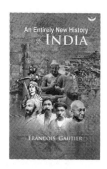

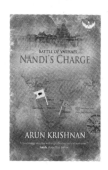

GARUDA PRAKASHAN BOOKS

GARUDA PRAKASHAN BOOKS

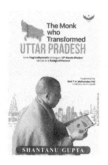
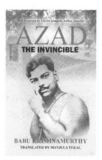

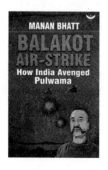

गरुड

Register:

Please register your book purchase at **grpr.in/register** to stay in touch and get informed about future books!

To order:

www.garudabooks.com

Follow us:

WEBSITE   : www.garudabooks.com

FACEBOOK : www.facebook.com/garudaprakashan/

TWITTER   : @garudaprakashan

INSTAGRAM : @garudabooks

YOUTUBE   : /garudabooks

Contact:

EMAIL   : contact@garudabooks.com

International queries:

EMAIL   : international@garudabooks.com

About the Author

Sunil is a software professional with over two decades of experience in the field of banking technology. Currently, he is working with Infosys in India in digital technologies, artificial intelligence, and start-up ecosystem. He has earlier worked with McKinsey, Accenture and I-flex solutions.

Sunil is an MBA from IIM-Lucknow and holds a BTech from IIT (ISM), Dhanbad.

Sunil has keen interest in writing, and he has previously authored best-selling books such as *Who Stole My Job, Transit Lounge* and *Who Stole My Time.*

Contacts

Facebook – https://www.facebook.com/Authorsunil

LinkedIn – https://www.linkedin.com/in/sunilkrmishra

Twitter – https://twitter.com/mishraksunil

Instagram – https://www.instagram.com/authorsunilmishra